THE LIVERPOOL BOYS ARE IN TOWN

[Revised Edition]

THE BIRTH OF TERRACE CULTURE

DAVE HEWITSON

Dedicated to;
My Wife Jeanette and two children Abby and Daniel.

With special thanks for words, photos and inspiration to:
my Dad, Angie and Robert Wade-Smith, John Connolly,
Neil Herron, Jay Montessori, Jamie Pike, Mark Platt @ LFCTV,
Ste Monaghan, Kev Sampson, Alan Hardwick, Peter Hooton,
Nicky Allt, Fitzy, Kev Lloyd, Eric Cull,
Gary Aspden @ adidas and Marcus Galley @ Mammoth Creative Works.

Published by 80s Casuals Ltd.
www.80sCasuals.co.uk
Design by Mammoth Creative Works

A catalogue record for this Book is available from the British Library.

Prologue

So how and why did Liverpool become integral in the development of this Youth Culture now acknowledged as being called 'Casuals'?

Maybe to find out we should trace a little bit of ancestry about the port and even our own forefathers. The answer could lie in our genes or even our parents' jeans.

It is a place that seems to stand alone at the end of the M62 looking out towards the ocean and far horizons with its back to the rest of the country. Its accent is quite rightly described as being 'exceedingly rare' and its culture certainly seems to take on a course of its own at times.

Liverpool has been a great Port since the 17th century. At that time the Cities Merchants developed a trade with America mainly due to its position on the Mersey which gave it an overwhelming advantage for trading with the New World. By the 1800s it was the main European Port and was known as the second City of the Empire.

The close links with the Atlantic slave trade was incontrovertible to the expansion and prosperity of the City. Profits from the trade were used on Buildings of a Grand scale and Liverpool was even known as "The New York of Europe" due to its wealth and the Grandeur of many of these buildings. Outside of London Liverpool has more Grade I and Grade II listed Buildings than any other British City.

Throughout the centuries it is safe to assume that many Scousers would have been employed in the sea trade. By the 1900s the rite of passage for any school leaver was to serve time at sea. Travel seemed to be in the blood and a way of life.

My Father and his Father were Merchant Seaman, travelling all over the world on numerous ships from the 1920s through to the 1960s. My Father would regale me with tales of jumping ship in Australia, being deported from Italy, bringing back Rock 'n' Roll records from the United States and Australia. Even seeing the great Louis Armstrong perform in Buenos Aires as well as watching a film on the same bill, 'The Wild One' with Marlon Brando. A movie of teenage angst that was banned in the UK until 1967. It was thought by then that the passage of time would have reduced its impact and relevance on teenagers.

At the age of 15 most school leavers longed to join 'the Merch' and set sail into the unknown. Dad would become one of many with tales to tell, but until recently they were kept mainly close to family and friends. No wonder I wanted to travel when I got older. My chance would arrive with ventures to far off lands with the mighty Reds but more of that later because my father's words are not just a passing tale. His and others like him have their own adventures to tell.

Tales that could only be told in Liverpool, similar to my own of following Liverpool F.C. In terms of Youth Cultures, his and those like him developed their own inimitable Style and Culture.

The 1950s are famous for Teddy Boys becoming the first Youth movement. But at a similar time and possibly a bit earlier the 'Cunard Yanks' were the forerunners of a teenage explosion yet to come to these shores. From the late 40s through to the early 60s 25000 seamen [mainly Scousers] sailed from Liverpool across the Atlantic working as catering staff, waiters, cooks and stewards. They worked for the Cunard Shipping Line and became affectionately known as the 'Cunard Yanks' due to the ships main port of call being New York, Boston, and further up North, Halifax and Montreal.

The prime focus of any Culture is the fashion, style and music. These guys had all three ingredients in abundance. Comparisons with the Liverpool fans travelling around Europe collecting exciting European sports and designer wear run parallel with the Cunard Yanks and Merchant Seamen on trips to New York and beyond. They became pioneers just like ourselves a generation later. In the early 50s the City of Liverpool was scarred from war and the fashions were drab to say the least. A mix of blacks, browns and greys. Fashion was most definitely in a rut. New York on the other hand had a magnetic pull, its interior of bright lights attracted many.

In 1851 the 'Bankers Magazine' described Liverpool as the New York of Europe and vice versa, New York being described as the Liverpool of the Americas. How apt that a century later these teenagers Style would be described as similar to those New York Stars of the big screen, Frank Sinatra and Tony Curtis. Their parents' ambition, dress and attitude were rejected in favour of Americana. Bringing back pieces of America unavailable back home. If it wasn't available in New York it wasn't available anywhere and we're not just talking about clothes here. Consumer goods including washing machines and fridge freezers were loaded onto the ship for the ships electrician to convert the electric current for UK use.

Stepping from the ship in New York Harbour was like stepping into another world. It was so easy to be sucked into this new Cultural explosion. One Cunard Yank described Britain as being in Black and White while the Big Apple was in Technicolor [American spelling]. It's an analogy I sometimes use myself to describe our visits to Europe in the late 70s and early 80s when Britain was blighted with recession with over 3 million unemployed. To us Britain was still in Black and White, the clothing and footwear was drab yet Europe seemed to be like a coloured T.V. with a hue of coloured polo shirts, tracksuits and coloured trainers.

Suits were the order of the day in the 50s and the Sinatra Style three button Suits were un-heard of back in the U.K. Lightweight materials and lighter in colour than anything back home, the styles were 15 years ahead of their time.

It wasn't only Suits though. Hats, Ox-Blood Moccasins, Ties, Cufflinks, even after-shave, anything that would make them stand out. When they returned the girls would say 'The ships are in', their style was so unique and noticeable. The hairstyle was Tony Curtis. The look was American.

My dad would bring back jeans, Levi and Wrangler, another surefire way of distinguishing a seaman. A craze for denim was about to begin on Merseyside.

Demand for such clothing attire began to grow throughout the 50s in Liverpool. Seamen returned to Liverpool laden with black market goods to sell to family and friends. American magazines were also brought back so that the local Tailors could copy the American styles. Entrepreneurism was encouraged and was to become a tradition within the city.

Besides the usual clothes, anything from double-door fridge freezers to record players had a market value. One guy had to leave his fridge freezer in the back yard, plugged in through the window, because it was too big to fit through an English width doorway. The Salvation Army thrift store in Manhattan was often the first port of call when docking, to stock up on white goods at a knock down price. These household goods were something the middle classes of Britain had not even seen as yet, but here was the working class youth of Liverpool living the high-life. Dressing better and living a more comfortable lifestyle than many of their elders.

The Cunard Yanks would also have you believe they had a hand in the Beatles sound. George Harrison purchased a second hand electric guitar from one. Apparently it was one of only two electric guitars in Liverpool at the time. The guy still has a signed £20 I.O.U. because George didn't have the full £90 cash on him at the time. I suspect this is now worth more than the original £20 he was owed. John Lennon was also believed to have purchased American records from returning sailors.

Music raced through their veins. New sounds first heard in the Jazz Clubs of NY plus local radio stations playing Doo-Wop, Blues and Country and Western meant the Seamans' musical tastes knew no boundaries. I remember as a kid playing my dads old 45s purchased from the U.S. and even Australia long before they were released in the U.K. He purchased a record player in Australia whilst on a sojourn during a 14 month trip. The self-made entertainment on the ships often included nights sitting around the record player.

By 1961 the grand ocean liners were giving way to air travel. The quicker way of crossing the Atlantic meant the liners demand diminished, also meaning employment on such vessels became less frequent. My father disembarked one last time to take up a job with Fords, but his tales had planted a seed and the draw and pull of Foreign Lands would once again have an impact on the youth of this city.

A generation on from my fathers' adventures at sea, Liverpool F.C. are conquering Europe and together we embark on a journey by train to see our beloved team pick up the first of many European Cups. Two days by train via Belgium, Germany and Switzerland to the final destination of Rome in 1977 has this 14 year old observing a new foreign world for the first time. A world with such an extreme palette of colour and style in comparison with the restrained look of Blighty that I would hunger for more of the same.

It didn't matter that I had to sell my Raleigh Chopper for £30 in the Echo to finance the trip. My dads mate lost his job after being told he wasn't welcome back if he went to the game. It was one of many similar stories centred around the desire to see Liverpool pick up their first European Cup.

Over the next 8 years we would be spoilt as Liverpool enjoyed the most productive period in its history with trips to Europe happening on a frequent scale. Holland, Germany, Switzerland, Belgium, Portugal, Italy and Spain were all stamped into the passport as myself and a new generation of travellers began an insatiable quest for the new. As everyone should already know this period would lead to a new Youth Culture being born, that of the 'Casual'. Fila, Sergio Tacchini and adidas, to name just a few became wardrobe staples during this time of Transalpino trips to the Continent to pick up such brands unavailable in the UK.

This amazing sense of personal style was running through our veins and this story has now been told on numerous occasions but what the 'Casual' did do was change the British High Street forever. Sportswear became everyday wear. Designer goods aimed at the upper classes are now so popular it verges on ubiquity. Every town is now saturated with Sports Stores while Designer has become mainstream.

The Liverpool obsession with Fashion and Style has always been the foundation of its wardrobe from those seamen of the 50s through to the 80s Casuals. Its not until you reach a certain midlife that you realise how influential your parents have been in the building of your own life. I suppose the first influence, which you don't really have a say in, is 'your team'.

We moved from the Anfield area, to Norris Green, when I was aged seven but I can still remember minding cars outside the house on match day. This would be whilst my Dad would wander off to the game with his mates, but I was too small to go.

The roar from the Kop could be heard as we played football in and out of the parked cars.

My Dad did take me to Burnley on a Boxing Day in 1969 aged 6 though. Come to think of it, my earliest memories of going the game seem to be of other trips on Boxing Day to Manchester City. Maybe that was my Mothers only day off all year and if dad was going the game then so was I.

So as the 1970s come around, the only games I'm allowed to go, besides those on Boxing Day, are the European Home games. Maybe it was easier to get tickets to sit as we always ended up in the Main Stand. An Alun Evans hat trick against Bayern Munich in the 1971 Fairs Cup isn't going to be forgotten even though I was only 8 years old. Momentous nights seemed an inevitability on these great evenings. Who can forget the 1973 UEFA Cup Final. [The old Fairs Cup came under the realm of UEFA in 1971, hence the name change.] An abandoned first leg at Anfield, due to a waterlogged pitch, with a replay of the game on the following day. We didn't have tickets for either game due to my Sister being hospitalised in Alder Hey but on the night of the replayed game I pleaded with my Dad to take me, as it was only 10p to get in. He hadn't heard of that and thought it was a ploy to go, so we had to visit the hospital. On returning home in the car I was again pleading. It's amazing how annoying a 10 year old can be until he gets his way. So we dropped off my Mother and other siblings before heading to the ground.

We arrived at the ground just before Half-Time and were able to get into the Kop through the Half-Time gate for 5p each. My first time ever on the Kop and it's a European Final. We stood at the very back and I remember being on his shoulders at one point but the noise and atmosphere became overwhelming and terrifying and I asked to be lowered. We won the game 3-0 due to some tactical intuition by the great man that is Bill Shankly. John Toshack being selected for the game due to his aerial prowess. A 0-2 defeat in Germany wasn't enough for us to lose a grip on the trophy and a Victory Parade through the streets of Liverpool soon followed.

The following year we beat Stromsgodset and I remember some young kids asking us the score on the way home. '11-0' my dad said, 'Piss off, mister' came the response. It really was 11-0 though and nine different players scored.

Other glory nights included seeing Neeskens and Cruyff playing for Barcelona. We drew 1-1 but would progress to the Final with a 1-0 win in Spain. These were World Class players you would only usually see on TV during World Cup Tournaments.

Then there was the Bruges, UEFA Cup Final. 0-2 down at Half Time and a Belgium brass band in the Paddock blaring away until three second half goals silenced their clamorous tones. The scene had been set. Liverpools history of travel and its Culture of Sport and Fashion were to become ingrained into the psyche of a new generation of teenagers like myself. We wanted to travel abroad like our Forefathers and we wanted to witness our football team engage in moments of glory that we could regale to our Sons in future years.

And so we come to the watershed year of 1977, which brings about another glory run with the club playing its first European Cup Final to be staged in Rome. En-route a Quarter Final trip to St Etienne in the sunny climes of Southern France leave an indelible mark. The well-dressed locals have a somewhat 'panache' about their style. Sporting short sleeve Polo Shirts in an array of bright hues along with slim jeans and boating shoes, the local youth are dressing for the weather without worry of the latest fashions.

My first European Away trip is to the Eternal City for the Final. A two-day journey on one of the many Special trains commissioned to take some of the 26000+ supporters who would be making the expedition to Rome.

My Raleigh Chopper got sold to fund the trip but a broken collar bone meant sitting up-right all the way there and back whilst others slept in luggage racks or across seats and floors. Playing football in the local park on the Saturday after the F.A. Cup Final had seen me re-enact the Jimmy Case goalscoring turn, only to end up on my back nursing a broken collar bone. After being strapped up in Alder Hey there was no way I'd be missing a first European Cup final. A 3-1 triumph meant this was to be the greatest day ever in Liverpool's history. We returned home, this time taking almost three days. We arrived on the Saturday having missed Tommy Smiths Testimonial the previous evening, but it mattered not. Of those who had made that arduous trip over Land and Sea, many would do the same again in the coming years as a new culture would begin to emerge, Fuelled by our fathers tales, Liverpool F.C. and a cheap European excursion travel company called...Transalpino.

FOREWORD. Things Have Changed

Contained in this book is an account of one lad's growing up in Merseyside that gives an insight into an era that is probably unimaginable to most twenty first century youths. As the author Dave once told me, 'I was advised that you can't go far wrong writing a book if you keep it to your own experiences'.

In Britain it was an era of three TV channels (that shut down before midnight), no home computers, no internet, football terracing (without stewards), no McDonalds, no compact discs, no DVD's (no videos for that matter), no CCTV cameras, no mobile phones, no iPods (or Walkmans), no Supermodels, no Stone Island (or Stone Roses), no Hip Hop, no Acid House, no eBay, no Gore-Tex, no men's Style magazines, no crack, no HIV, no ecstasy, pizzas no bigger than 6" and no retrospectives. An era where Glastonbury was for Hippies and corporate sponsorship of music festivals was unheard of. An era where European Designer clothing brands were off the radar to regular punters. An era where every lad in the UK called their sports shoes trainers rather than 'sneakers'.

Clothes, Music and Football were a great way to escape the mundanity of being a working class teenager in the rainy North West (the first episode of 'One Summer' is a great reminder of how dull it was).

Where I was from me and my mates generally bought our trainers from small independent Sports Shops that were often owned by retired Sportsmen – Sports Shoes were sold alongside tennis rackets, cricket bats, goalkeepers gloves and yet to be engraved trophies. It wasn't until about 1982 (I was born in 1969) that I became aware of older lads making the exodus to Switzerland and Austria (where the adidas were displayed in pairs!!!). Unlike Liverpool F.C., Blackburn Rovers never made it into Europe back then but their supporters certainly did.

This book is a snapshot from the beginnings of a very British phenomenon that has been widely misunderstood, in many cases inaccurately documented (I was at the Hacienda all-dayer in '85 Phil), and categorised with labels that somehow don't quite sit right with me. The word 'Scally' in 2008 evokes images of snotty nosed, hooded car thieves with novelty socks tucked into shellsuit pants. Alternatively 'Casuals' seems to have become the defining name but even that is still rejected by many – a word that was born out of the South being used to label a movement that grew out of the North? Is it any wonder it makes some people uncomfortable?

A few years ago I was asked by an American lady to try and explain what a 'Casual' is – after ten minutes of tying myself in verbal knots trying to explain I realised through no fault of her own she could never truly understand. There is nothing comparable in American culture (not that I am aware of anyway) – Gangbangers? Homeboys? Jocks? Nerds? Hipsters?. . . No chance. The reference points simply don't exist in the States. Loyal football supporters who wouldn't be seen dead in their team's shirt? Work that one out. People who don't see the beauty of shoes with pegs in the sole are never going to truly understand.

At the time no Documentaries were made about what was happening on the terraces in the North West and very few photos were taken (outside of holiday snaps and pics taken at the odd away fixture). Magazines were oblivious to it – when Kevin Sampson pitched an idea for an article about it to The Face in 1982 his idea was initially turned down (their response implied that they thought it was a small, insignificant scene), A year later they were all over it. By the time people started to write about it the whole thing had grown well beyond the confines of Liverpool and Manchester.

Unlike most other British youth movements the bands that were popular at the time hardly resembled their 'Scally' following (although coincidentally Talking Heads were sporting Lacoste polo shirts when they played 'Psycho Killer' on the Whistle Test).

Over the years I've thought a lot about how under exposed this movement has been outside of the U.K. in comparison to the likes of Punk Rock, 2 Tone, Skinheads, etc. A style can easily be appropriated – a mentality can't. The constantly evolving look (particularly from 79-89), different brands and the one-upmanship that drove the whole thing meant that there was never a defining look that could be imitated. To add to the confusion, post 1983 most Towns and Cities across the UK had picked up on it and each was adding their own unique twist on the style. Whilst it may never translate into the cultures of other Countries it has without doubt inspired and informed much of British men's fashion for the past 30 years.

I didn't consider it at the time but there was something anti-establishment in our adopting designer brands that somehow felt like that they weren't meant for us. It was all about the context. I'll never forget the look on the manager's face in 'Wardrobe' ('gentleman's outfitters') in Blackburn when we used to turn up on the doorstep of his shop. He made the mistake of being Blackburn's only Armani stockist in the early 80s. He was busy trying to make his living selling expensive Italian knitwear and suits to wealthy businessmen – he didn't anticipate the alternative audience this would attract. As he and his affluent clientele stood around the shop's open log fire drinking tea he would be besieged by legions of cheeky teenagers asking to see the sweaters with the eagle on. He hated us.

In the era of 12-month passports and cheap European rail travel I was in awe of the suede and leather 3 stripe masterpieces that the geniuses in Herzogenaurach gave us. I now feel that there was something oddly befitting about the city names stamped onto the sides of the shoes – Munchen, Stockholm, Amsterdam, Zurich – these gave them a European slant and somehow reflected the spirit of the times. It was liberating to know that there was a world beyond redundancies, Thatcherism, unemployment figures and YTS schemes. It was a world I was determined to access at the first opportunity.

I am happy that through its support of Mr. Hewitsons' projects adidas has been able to acknowledge the fact that for better or for worse the world described in this book (and its fashion) has an indisputable role in its rich and colourful history. It is a scene that adidas never targeted or set out to be a part of but somehow unwittingly ended up at its very centre.

Gary Aspden / adidas
February 2008

> "No amount of marketing spend or know how could create the inextricable link that adidas has with the Culture of the British Football Terraces."

Absolute Beginners

So it's a visit to Wembley Stadium in the August of 1977. The occasion being the Charity Shield between Liverpool and Manchester United. A hundred thousand fans sauntered up Wembley Way, but before the football had even begun something had caught the eye outside the Stadium.

Sitting on the steps close to the turnstiles are twenty or so young lads. Teenagers between the ages of 15 and 17 years old. Many people glance over, unsure as to where they are from. Were they Scousers or Mancs? They sit nonchalantly unaware of the interest they are creating. Some are sporting a strange new hairstyle, effeminate in look but there was nothing feminine about the attitude and confidence transmitting from this gang. Attired in straight jeans or cords, which just aren't the order of the day, they are also wearing adidas sports trainers, again not common in an era of disco and punk fashion.

Approximately two months later and the venue has changed to Elland Road, Leeds. Liverpool are the visitors and in a decade of crowd violence there is trouble at the game. After the match there is stand-off in the car park. Liverpool's very own Kop Bootboys had just attacked this same group of lads seen previously on those Wembley steps. Mistaking them as Leeds supporters because of the difference in their clothes, it's not until a few on opposite sides recognise each other that the fighting stops and everyone bursts out laughing. A defining moment if ever there was one.

Times were changing. Going to the match would never be the same again, it was no longer just about the football and a bit of scrap, it was now also about the clothes and the attitude. A whole new Youth Culture was emerging and these Absolute Beginners were there at the start. Flared jeans had been laid to rest as far as this new wave of fashionable youth were concerned. Liverpool's first European cup triumph in Rome would be the last time so many flared jeans and club colours would be worn by so many of these Scouse hordes.

1977 was the defining year. Yes, Punk was becoming a mainstream phenomena and also an inspiration on Merseyside as Teenagers transformed their wardrobes by acquiring straight jeans, usually Lois or Levis, combined with Jelly (see through plastic) Sandals and a mohair jumper, but by its Winter these kids, many of whom were still in school, were asking their parents for adidas Samba and the adidas ST2 Cagoule. The satiable appetite for adidas had started. Everyone already owned the Originals Trefoil Logo T-Shirt with the stripes running down the shoulder. I have a photo from one of my family holidays in North Wales in the mid 70s that has myself and two cousins in different coloured versions, Yellow, Sky Blue and White.

Surprisingly the local Sports Store wasn't the only place that you could purchase the latest look. My mother had a few Catalogues, Empire, Gratton and Littlewoods, from which she would take orders and collect a small commission. It was in one of these that I first noticed the Adidas ST2 Cagoule. Navy with a red inner and lightly padded I had to have one. By November I had one in my possession and before long four mates were asking me if my ma would order one for them. Our first purchase by HP (Hire Purchase) and a saviour in our quest to stay relevant in the fashion stakes. It was at this point, aged 14, that I thought that my Pocket Money wouldn't be enough to keep up with local trends. I delivered papers of a Sunday which paid better than a daily round because the papers were heavier, plus a job on the milk round during holidays paid handsomely for trips to Anfield and the odd piece of clothing or trainers.

1978/79

By the 1978/79 years, the new Culture, first noticed at Wembley the previous year, was now gaining momentum on Merseyside. It went totally un-documented nationally for approximately another 5 years. Maybe this had something to do with it being Northern based. The daily papers only noticed the hooligan element and there weren't many Mens Magazines filling the shelves to spread the news. At first, no name was attached to this group. Words such as Smoothies, Straights, Squares and Scallys were banded about. At the time, all sorts of styles were walking the streets and so if you weren't a Mod or maybe a Punk, then you were a Straight or Square. It was a title to distinguish an ordinary teenager who looked like he/she knew how to dress smart. Scallys were those youngsters up to no good. A name still used to this day that conjures up images of a Liverpool rogue.

In 1983, the Face magazine published an article mentioning the 'Casuals' look. This now seems to be the word used by all. In Liverpool, the word doesn't account for much as it had never been used at the time and it appeared to be some Southern reporter putting a title on a bunch of 15-year-old Cockney kids. The Culture had, by this time, been well and truly put on the map by the travelling hordes of Liverpool and Everton Supporters.

These years saw the City streets a mix of 25 years of Youth Culture. Probe and X-Stremes Arcade on Button Street were awash with a new generation of Teds and Rockabilly's. Mods have also re-surfaced with the new film Quadrophenia glorifying the cause. Skinheads also came back, Donkey Jackets and Airwear at the ready. Punk was new to the scene, but had been making a show for a year or two on Button Street and in one or two clubs [The Swinging Apple and Erics] in the City centre. Anyone leaving school at this time would be spoilt for choice. The teenager's time had come.

Besides these different styles the kids in Liverpool were about to create their own unique outlook on taste. A Culture all of their own that in years to come would be labelled 'Casual'. It would spread Nationally, in the same way that the original Teddy Boys of the fifties spread from the South End of London. This was different though, it wasn't London setting a trend for the rest of the Country to follow. Liverpool was having a Cultural revolution all of its own and there was a buzz about the place that had not been seen since the heyday of The Beatles and the Merseybeat era of the early sixties.

Nowadays you only have to pick up one of the latest Men's Magazines to get an idea of what is fashionable and what to wear. Not so in 1978. The closest thing to these Magazines at the time would be the NME's pages of stylish Indie bands and the latest adverts in the back pages for London clothes shops. Monthly style magazines were for women only. Liverpool would have its own perception on style and what to wear.

1978 was to be a watershed year. It was the year every kid, boy and girl, in every school and on every street corner wanted a strange girlie haircut. The Wedge was synonymous with the Casual look. A haircut that would set Liverpool apart from every other city for a few years. It was a style that stood out. It meant travelling to an away game with the mob so as not to be singled out by opposing fans. Travelling by car was definitely not recommended. The look was totally Scouse, a Wedge, a pair of Lois Jeans, and a pair of Adidas Samba on the feet. Scousers stood out, but that was the point. We were dressing better than everyone else, being different and far superior than everyone else, plus we had the best team in Europe. Also, the Liverpool music scene was about to take off. Eric's was one of the top Clubs in the Country at the time and it had a group of members who aspired to be musicians and who would become future top 20 selling artists. There wasn't a better place to live for the teenagers of the time. Football, Fashion and Music. Liverpool had the lot.

The kids walking around today in their designer tracksuits with their hands down the front of their pants, have no idea that before this period, trainers and tracksuits were for people who actually did sport. Sports shops were few and far between and sold mainly gear for cricket, athletics and tennis etc. The Training Shoes were for just that.....Training. Whether it be Football, Tennis or Squash.

The Casual would redefine how a generation of kids would dress for the next 40 years or more. The style developed over the next three years to encompass International Sportswear and would make millionaires out of entrepreneurial geniuses. Within three years, the Liverpool street Culture that had started with having a pair of jeans from Greaty [Great Homer Street Market] before everyone else now meant having a pair of trainees only available from Germany or a tracksuit from Italy that was impossible for anyone else to get. That was unless you travelled abroad on shopping expeditions. Following Liverpool would enable you to kill two birds with one stone, support the team and return with an array of goodies unavailable in the U.K. 1981 was a European Cup winning year for Liverpool F.C. and trips to Munich Germany and Paris France, plus friendlies in Germany and Switzerland would see many Scousers returning with Head Bags full of adidas, Fila and the like to wear themselves or sell on to friends.

The following year of 1982 would also see a certain Robert Wade Smith open a small shop on Slater Street to sell adidas trainers that he himself brought back from Germany. The shop would eventually expand and move to bigger premises to sell many European brands and keep up with the ever-growing need for Designer Sportswear. Wade Smith became the first retail outlet in Europe to sell just Designer Sportswear.

So this wasn't just a group of kids following fashion and wearing the latest trends, these kids were creating their own Trends and Style. The clothes, the attitude and ultimately the match defined the Culture. Every Culture has its own lifestyle.

'A Way of Life' was how Mods described their Culture and it was the same for us. It was how you lived your life day to day and what you did to define that Culture. Liverpool teens through each generation would follow different lifestyles to their predecessors. An interest in the look and the liking for a particular type of music had always contributed to the style of the times whether it be Teds, Mods, Skins etc. However a football orientated lifestyle was how the Casual would live. Going to the game whether it be home or away would mean putting on your best gear and walking with a swagger with your hands sometimes clasped behind the back. It was where you could witness the latest jeans, trainers and jackets. Wellknown faces, that would be seen at most away games and in Europe, would appear in the newest of exclusive styles. The streets around Anfield and also Goodison became a living catwalk. A Fashion Show for any visiting away fans and those who had still yet to travel.

The Lure Of The Well Turned Out Mob

Looking back at this period of self-indulgent hedonism for status symbols, it also become appropriate of the time for the Terraces to become a statement of ones own identity and personality. A penchant for individuality would lead this new breed of style aficionados away from Liverpool's famous Kop, into a separate stand to set up camp. An endearing aura of cool accompanied the move and before long numbers swelled into a mainstream trend. What happened at Liverpool possibly happened at most grounds around the country.

It's true to say that by the late 70s the Kop was losing its charm to some. A nascent rival was emerging, in the form of the Anfield Road End. There had been no conflict between the Kop and the Anfield Road during the 70s, you made your choice and stood wherever to cheer on the Mighty Reds. At one time it was possible to walk around from one end of the ground to the other, so you could stand in a position that Liverpool were attacking. Standing on the Kop had been something to aspire to, not revolt against. That was until the start of the 1977/78 season when a conflict of lifestyle aspirations began to set in. The fashion gripping Merseyside and the image being formed wasn't coming from Carnaby Street or the catwalks of London but the Terraces of the Anfield Road. The Terraces became the fashion catwalk. Straight jeans and trainees had been given the seal of approval.

Flared jeans had become an embarrassing anachronism. Suddenly the Kop had also become that. The kids were looking for their own identity and the appeal of the Road End was having an impact that would reverberate throughout the fashion world for years to come.

'A divide was now being driven between the Kop and the Road End. The lads going into the Anfield Road were mainly Scouse and the lure of the well-turned out mob had the numbers growing by the week. It was the place to be seen and to catch up on the latest fashions. The Kop was now for the older generation, plus the badly dressed out of towners or woolly-backs as they were known, many of whom were disgusted at the actions of these local ruffians. The rift between the two sets of supporters was to last for up to six years. Tit for tat exchanges in song done nothing to help quell the distaste.

While the Kop seemed slow on the up-take in the fashion stakes, the Road End Boys were setting standards for the rest of the Country to follow. Liverpool's success in Europe had these style revolutionaries liberating the Continent of the best in Designer Sportswear and adidas trainees. Ownership ensured instant kudos amongst fellow Road Enders and friends alike. Between the years of '77 and '83 an indelible mark had been left on the consumer world. Designer sports shops began opening in every city to feed the growing band of youth now known as 'Casuals'. By the 1982/83 season each and every Club had its own firm of Casual dressed supporters inspired by the Annie Road elite. For many though, the style was now plummeting into mass mediocrity, even the Kop was beginning to look well dressed.

It looked like the conflict of interests was subsiding as more and more pioneers of the previous years began drifting back to the Kop. Their contribution to Modern Culture had definitely been asserted and the Road End now had as much a part of Liverpool Football Clubs history as the Kop or any other part of the ground.

Even during this period of Road End dominance the allure of the Kop on a European night attracted most. Its DNA was in every Liverpool supporter. The Kop would be at its most vocal and was certainly a potent force other teams supporters could only dream about. It also had its own Cultural value, a value embracing authenticity, a provenance of originality with its vociferous, witty support, something which should never be lost.

Although hooliganism had been around since the sixties, by the late seventies it had escalated enough for 22 European ministers to hold a 3 day meeting in April 1978 in London 'to clean up sport' with particular attention being paid to football hooliganism. This was no worry to the teenagers attending games at this time though. Fighting at the match had become a part of the Culture. The whole scene seemed to centre around the match, whether it was a home or away game. Meeting before the game, attending the game and the after match shenanigans would play its part. Meeting up with the mates on a Saturday night would mean discussing the day's events over a game of pool in Daley's [Daley's Dandelion] and a few pints in Scarletts Bar or Maxwells Plum.

Music didn't really influence the scene. Going out at the weekend meant visiting a few certain Pubs and Clubs. In the early days The Swinging Apple, Checkmate and Michelle Claires were popular and then The Harrington came to the fore with its mix of punk, new wave and electronic music which was more appealing than the disco sounds being touted in most other clubs. Disco was at it's height in 1978 and Scamps on Brownlow Hill was advertising in the Echo for everyone to catch the new sensation of 'Saturday Night Fever', but this was 'too popular' for the new breed.

If you wanted to be different from everyone else you also wanted to listen to new music before most, so the aforementioned Pubs and Clubs with their up-to-the-minute DJ's and jukebox's enabled this.

The Punks around at the time influenced many venue's to allow people in without a jacket and tie, which was the norm for Clubs like Tuxedo Junction and Ugly's. However, smart casual attire would gain entrance to all pubs plus places like The Swinging Apple, The Harrington and Erics. Shoes were necessary though. So, in the space of three years Pod, College and eventually the ever-popular Kickers would be the shoe to wear. The school teenager would also need shoes for school so there was always a certain shoe that was the latest style to be seen in.

Within the space of a couple of years, this new Culture would expand to encompass visits to Europe to find new Designer labels unavailable back home. A thriving black market arose in firstly adidas trainers and then almost anything that came from Italian sportswear giants such as Fila, Sergio Tacchini, Robe di Kappa and Ellesse etc. Tracksuits, T-Shirts and Jumpers would all fetch good money back home. Eventually anything with a top label would make a nice profit.

The Wedge Hairstyle

As the years pass and history has become somewhat clouded, the roots of the Casual will be forever argued about in Pubs and Clubs up and down the land. The main fact is Liverpool would adopt a hairstyle that had its roots in the Soul music of the time. The Soul fraternity in South London had adopted the wedge, but on Merseyside a David Bowie / Bryan Ferry influence was to have a hold on the Youth. Style icon Bryan Ferry's Roxy Music had appeared at The Empire on Lime Street in 1977 and had a Greatest Hits album out at the time. Bowie on the other hand had just released the 'Low' album and had three top 30 singles.

On the cover of the 'Low' album Bowie was sporting a Wedge haircut that would inspire many. The image being taken from a still frame from his appearance in the film 'The Man Who Fell To Earth'. The album itself was a commercial success, reaching Number 2 in the UK Charts. Kept off the Top Spot by American Country star Slim Whitman. But it was that hairstyle that elevated the album to iconic status.

My Mrs, Jeanette, remembers going to an under 18's Disco at Tiffany's Club near the Pier Head on a Sunday afternoon. 'Everyone had a Wedge hairstyle and the favourite music played would be classic Bowie and Roxy Music. I was still at school at the time, so it would have been 1978. Everyone called it 'The Roxy Music Disco'. There was another under 18's disco at the Lord Nelson on most Sunday nights with a mix of match going lads 'Into the Scene' plus the regular Roxy/Bowie lookalikes. Often the night ended in violence between both sets of fans.

Under 18 Discos were quite common around Liverpool at the time but many seemed to be a source of confrontation between different regions of the City. Erics was the main club in town for the new up and coming groups and on most Saturday afternoons a matinee for the under 16's would be held. Alcohol free of course. Once the young teenagers were able to get into proper clubs, Michelle Claires and Checkmate soon became the main ones to listen to the music. The Swinging Apple, which was predominantly a Punk Club, was another favourite. A mix of Punks, Skinheads and match lads, the Apple satisfied most with a mix of it's Punk, Reggae and New Wave Music.

Besides Bowie and Ferry, there was another group whom this crowd endeared and that was Liverpool's very own Deaf School. Lead by the enigmatic Bryan Ferry disciple Enrico Cadillac, he of the quiffy wedge. The adoring fans here had someone of style whom they could adhere to. Having taken their name from the rehearsal rooms, the group would release three albums between 1976 and 1978 but never hit the big time. On Merseyside, this made them more endearing and wonderful. Scousers love the feeling of 'This is ours and no-one else's'. It was the same with the trainers and clothes.

Being in Liverpool, you were either a Red or a Blue. So the night clubs were being frequented by a football going crowd as well as your student types who liked dressing up like their heroes. Baggy trousers known as Bowie Pants became popular but no one was going to turn up at Anfield or Goodison in a pair. Therefore, the football followers started their own take on the fashion. The pants being replaced by jeans or cords and the shoes by trainers or suedies.

At the time the Soul boys down South had taken to wearing mohair jumpers, pegged trousers or leather pants with jelly sandals. They would frequent a club called 'The Lacy Lady' and this style of dress would form the first basic look of Punks. Many Punks in years to come spoke of visiting The Lacy Lady.

In Liverpool however, the Soul look wouldn't last, the summers attire of mohair and jelly sandals would be replaced with a winter of small collared shirts, Lois Jeans, Cords or Canvas, available in black, and so ideal for school, and the ubiquitous adidas Samba. Together with the Wedge, the lads on Merseyside would at first be called Straights or Squares, but many Cockneys visiting Anfield or Goodison could be heard shouting 'Soul boys where's your scarves?'

Returning to the Wedge, the style was invented by Trevor Sorbie at the Vidal Sassoon salon in London in 1974. It would be the first hairstyle to feature in a two-page spread in Vogue. A lop-sided style with a side part, short on one side with an extra long fringe to the other. The fringe growing down to cover the eye in many cases. The hair would have to be flicked up out of the eye to be able to see, hence the nickname 'the flick'. The back would be graduated.

Soulboys would have you believe a stylist by the name of Ricci Burns invented the cut, but this is open to debate much like the origins of most Cultures. One thing is for certain, the cut was styled with women in mind. In America a woman by the name of Dorothy Hamill would choose the look for the 1976 Winter Olympics. She was to become an American sweetheart and the most recognised athlete in America when she unexpectedly won gold. She signs a contract with Clairol and suddenly every woman in the U.S. would take on the look.

This side of the Atlantic though, the look had crossed over from the pages of Vogue to the Soul Clubs of London and the Terraces of Merseyside. Herbert was the owner of the hairdressers 'Herberts' on Church Street. He opened his first salon in the suburbs of Liverpool in 1963 and soon established himself in the city with numerous hair salons, beauty salons, a restaurant, three gents' boutiques and a few other successful enterprises including the Hollywood Night Club on Duke Street. His hair salons would be where he would skilfully pioneer the Wedge style as a Liverpool cut for the masses. Herbert explains in his own inimitable way, 'Although the Wedge was a woman's cut it could be done in a masculine way.

The time was right. I was the first person to highlight my hair back in the late sixties and I also introduced the perm to the Liverpool footballers. During the early days, men usually washed their hair with soap and the only aftershave besides Hai-Karate and Brut was your dads Old Spice. We became the first hairdressers to introduce a wash, cut and blow, and so eventually, men would start using shampoo and then more and more companies were introducing after shaves, colognes and deodorants. Men were now looking into their feminine side and the Wedge just tied in with the times. Our Wedge appeared in all the top magazines of the time. £5 plus tip was the going rate.' So there you go, Herbert was responsible for many teenagers looking into their feminine side.

Herberts became the main place to get your hair cut. Having introduced the Wedge to Liverpool, he was the main hairdresser in town whom everyone knew. He was a character in himself and most people knew of him because of the shops, club, hair salons and the fact that he drove around in a pink car and owned a pink house. Herbert 'I had a pink shirt which I always wore and I always said eventually many men would wear pink.' He wasn't far wrong in that within a few years Lacoste polo T-Shirts would be lapped up in numerous hues including pink and lemon. Hairdressers in Liverpool would soon be inundated with requests for the style. Herberts would even tell its clients about the look. Tony 'I went to Herberts and the stylist asked me if I would like it cut in a Wedge. I told her yes, although I had no idea what it was like, but for £5, she should know what was 'IN' or 'OUT'. It was only a few days later at an Everton match that I noticed two or three lads with the same style.' It wouldn't be long before this would be the only style to acquire.

Other hairdressers soon caught on. Girls were also sporting the latest style. Jeanette had the cut for a couple of months before her dad would cut the fringe off in a rage. He had grown sick of talking to her through one eye. 'I eventually got a fiver off him to get it re-styled in the salon downstairs in the X-Stremes Arcade'. The girls tended to comb their hair over from right to left and the boys vice versa.

In the first few months of this new hairstyle, it became increasingly difficult to recognise the boys from the girls from a distance, especially from behind. Girls had started sporting the same looks as well as hair. College shoes and Lois jeans were worn by all, the girls also went heavy on the jewellery with sovereigns on a neck-chain plus a sovereign ring matched with hoop earrings. The boys wore the sovereign ring or if they were well-off a Kruggerand.

The girlie style wasn't being taken to the night Clubs now, it had transferred to the Terraces of Anfield and Goodison. So, who would know if it had been a girl's hairstyle to start with? The Wedge would last a couple of seasons before things began to get out of hand with a few people letting the fringe grow abnormally long [Human League Phil Oakey style]. A mushroom bowl-head cut would replace the wedge but not for a few years yet. A new Culture was now beginning to take shape. The hairstyle was in place and so now the clothes. Jeans and Trainers would now grip the mass of youth seen congregating on the street corners in close proximity to the football grounds and in the local pubs.

She's a Liverpool Girl

As the latest fashions gripped the Liverpool scene, the girls weren't ones to be left behind. The wearing of a short kilt is fondly recalled by those old enough to have entered the Harrington at the start of this fashion phenomenon. The kilt craze caused such a furore that there would be a feature about it on Granada Reports.

In these early stages of manifestation the girls fashion mirrored the boys to the extent of wearing the same footwear and jeans. Pod, Kickers and College shoes with tassels were worn plus the same makes of jeans, Lois, Inega and F.U.'s. A favourite shop was Bus Stop on Cases Street for French Connection Stripey Sweatshirts. Greaty was always paid a visit to pick up Inega fitted shirts with a ruffled front, Inega black or red velvet jeans and the College shoes. A queue would form early doors for the tassled College that had a pointed toe and a stiletto heel.

For a night out on the town the jeans were replaced with pencil skirts. Toners semi permanent colours would be added to the hair. Burgundy being a favourite colour.

Jeanette mixed with the match lads and would even meet up at three quarter time to watch their exploits after the game. On the days when there was an away game she would mind their sovereigns and jewellery and meet them in town after the train arrived back in Lime Street. Most of her Job Creation money was spent on the fashions.

Although the match wasn't for girls, the Summer months would be spent with the lads on days out to Southport. Southport is a small seaside resort, not more than 20 miles from Liverpool. During the winter months, the rain and wind swept prom is deserted apart from the odd retiree walking his dog. There isn't much call to pay the Town a social visit. The Pleasureland Fairground is like a ghost town and the Swimming Baths are way too cold.

Come the Summer months though and the place comes alive. The Baths fill up and the car parks overflow with day-trippers, but best of all the fairground bustles with kids, fathers and mothers with prams, boys and girls queuing for the rides. Being a half hour train journey from Liverpool, Southport becomes a week-end mecca for Scouse teenagers determined to 'have a laugh.'

In the Summers of '79 and '80 the Scouse lads and girls who were into the fashion of the day would, as your Mother says, put on their Sunday best. It was an easy and enduring look of jeans with Pod, Kickers or Kios plus a nice T-Shirt or Shirt. Jeanette had the flick to die for [another necessity] and would meet up with the lads each weekend. 'We would meet up in town [Liverpool] and all get the train together. Some weeks there'd be about 30 or 40 of us. I remember one week I'd been going on at me mum to get me some new Kickers. I finally got a baby pink pair and wore them for the first time on the next excursion to Southport. I had my Kickers and a pair of white Inega jeans with a French Connection Check Shirt on. You had to get dressed up or you'd get the piss taken out of you all day. When we were at the fair, the caterpillar was for snoggin' because you could pull the covers over and no one would see you. The lads would then go into the funhouse and the girls would act as look-out to tell them if anyone was going in. As soon as anyone went in who wasn't a Scouser they'd get punched and kicked and threw about the place in the dark. This became a regular occurrence until one week when they had security patrolling inside the funhouse to stop 'them Scousers'. I think they even called the police on one occasion.'

The girls' fashion mirrored the lads from about '77 to '81, until the lads went off to liberate Europe of the finest of Sportswear and the girls fashion took on a separate route. These young Scallys were soon running around in Fila and Tacchini tracksuits while the girls went for a leather look, with leather jeans and skirts, which was closely followed by loose fitting jumpsuits.

Lois Jeans & Adidas Samba

Although the hairstyle had been transported from the Soul Clubs of London to Merseyside, the dress code would become decidedly home grown. Trainers had become the staple footwear to be seen in. They replaced Baseball Boots and Airwear as the newest fashion accessory. It wasn't just any pair though. adidas were the masters of sportswear in 1978. They had been endorsing highprofile Sportsmen during the 1970's and the Company had over 700 patents for footwear and equipment by the time of founder Adi Dasslers death in this year. Now they would come into their own on Merseyside. They had a variety of trainers out in the Sports Stores that would suit all pockets. The All-Black range were football trainers. Bamba, Mamba, and Samba were their names, Bamba being the cheapest because they were mainly plastic, with the all leather Samba being the most expensive at £19.99. Obviously, the Samba would have more appeal and status. This was the moment when a status symbol, in this case the expensive trainers that weren't available to all because of the price, began to define a growing youth culture. Investing in expensive luxury would ensure exclusivity. No one realised it at the time but it was to be the main objective of the Casual lifestyle for years to come. adidas Kick was also about at the time and many still fondly remember them as their first pair of trainees. They were cheaper than Samba, but Samba would capture the imagination. They would break all adidas records as the most sold pair of trainers in the brands history and the longest in production years.

If you were too young or didn't have enough money to afford the adidas, then your mother would probably get you a cheap pair of Mitre Memphis. Made in England, Mitre were worn by many Footballers at the time and even Muhammad Ali at one point, but although the quality may have been comparable to the adidas Samba, they wouldn't be an acceptable alternative with the fashionistas of the day.

At this time, Liverpool accounted for 30% of the total sales of adidas in the U.K. In the three year period of 1979 to the end of 1981 Top Man took in the region of £750,000 in adidas sales alone. No doubt having something to do with the trainer Culture developing.

The clothing styles would be available to all at first. It was just a matter of knowing where to go. Paul can still recall going for his first small-collared shirt. 'I can still remember going to All Mankind in Old Swan and getting a green and grey small collared check shirt. The Samba had to have the bubble [moulded] tongue and the only place I remember being able to get them at the time was downstairs in Heslop and Duckinfield on Stanley Street.' St. Johns Precinct had a few shops where it was possible to keep up with the latest trends at first. Places like MC Sports, Issy Crown, Gansgear, SMC Ltd [Shit Mens Clobber], Goldrush, Easywear Casuals and The Westerner would be the first places to get hold of certain jeans, small-collared shirts, stripey polos and T-shirts etc.

Tony remembers going to St. Johns Precinct. 'The Westerner was a store designed like a Wild West Saloon with swing doors. They sold mainly denim and so it was possible to get Lois Jeans and black Canvas for school.' Lois were the real giants of Spain and the only one of interest to the youth. A bull being the logo adorning the back label on the back of the jeans. The youngsters in the schools were quick to catch on to the newest of fads and wanted to show off their latest wear to their mates in class. The Lois Canvas with Pod or the College Loafer and a small collared shirt became regulation school wear. Soon these kids were no longer asking for an Atari Games Console or Star Wars Figures for Christmas. They now wanted adidas Trainers. Mums and Dads were now telling their kids they could have the most expensive pair of adidas as a Christmas present instead of a cheap pair with their Christmas clothes.

The Winter of 1978/79 had seen the very small-collared shirt, usually with a check design, became a staple item of dress. From the start of the 70s shirt collars had been embarrassingly large, but this new style was about to take hold.

Fashion was going from one extreme to another. Large collars to small, wide jeans to narrow, long hair to short etc. Obviously, the shirt had to be worn in a certain way. It became de-rigueur to wear the shirt with the top button fastened, no doubt keeping you warmer because not wearing a coat was the latest way to look Cool. This nearly had dire consequences at a Bolton/Liverpool game at Burnden Park on 1st May 1979 when a sudden cold spell with rain and snow would drown the away supporters on the open Railway Embankment End and eight fans in only shirts would need hospital treatment for exposure. Those who couldn't put up with this extraordinary British weather wore an adidas waterproof jacket. Blue with three white stripes down the sleeves, a red inner and a hidden hood in the collar. The adidas ST2 Cagoule was a Top Man favourite that sold 20000 in a two-year spell between 1979 and 1981. Either that or a green Peter Storm Cagoule. Peter Storm being the first to weld together the seams of complete jackets without stitching therefore providing '100% waterproof nylon rainwear'. The Cagoule was a firm favourite and is still fondly remembered.

A year earlier had seen the end of the Parkas reign. The green army surplus coat was practical, readily available and cheap. Its place in history was assured in the Mod days of the 1960s. The 70s saw the coat revived and being worn from Lands End to John O'Groats. On Merseyside we had to be different and opted for the blue version. Maybe with a Fred Perry or adidas T-Shirt underneath and the first straight leg Lois or Levi's. Donkey Jackets, Harringtons, Lumberjack Jackets and blue Snorkels all seemed to disappear overnight, being replaced by the adidas ST2 or Peter Storm Cagoules.

Around this same time, the acrylic Slazenger V-neck became ubiquitous. The jumper was embroidered with a panther on the left breast and usually worn with a t-shirt underneath. There will be a least one photo in every household of someone in a Slazenger Jumper. As with all of the clothing at the time, it was readily available and quite cheap.

Two years later, Made in Scotland Lambswool Pringle V-Necks would be worn in a similar way with a plain t-shirt, but the Pringle was a lot more expensive than Slazenger. It soon became apparent that the best place to find these would be in the Shop of your local Golf Club. They were produced for Golfers and this became a hint as to what was to come as the Casuals Wardrobe began to expand. Golfing Sweaters from Golf Shops, Mountaineering Jackets such as Berghaus and Ski Jumpers from Mountain Sports Stores. If you were looking for Sportswear it was obvious these Sporting Stores would be carrying the stock.

Pod, College Shoes, Kickers & Kios

By the Summer of 1979, College shoes bought from Great Homer Street Market (Greaty) or Ravel were the shoes to be seen in. College were a loafer style slip-on shoe with a metal bar (horse bit) across the front with the word college engraved on it. Another style had two tassels on the front. Many kids would be up and out by 8.00 a.m. on a Saturday morning to jump the bus down to Greaty to get a pair before they sold out. The shoes were worn by both sexes, as were Kickers the following year. The ugly Pod [Product of Desire] shoe was also having its time. Pod had only been around since the Summer of 1976 but the company's expansion of retail outlets soon saw the name become well known nationally. It wasn't long before they caught on in Liverpool. The ones with the paratrooper sole being the most sought after. Available from Harold Ian on Lime Street or Heroes on Mount Pleasant. Both were soon to be put in the shadows by the much revered Kickers.

1980 saw chaos reign as shops sold out of the shoe as soon as they came in. Kickers originated in 1970 France after Daniel Raufast wanted to design a shoe to wear with jeans. They seemed to be the most expensive shoe on the market. Around £30 from Close Encounters in St Johns Market, these colourful shoes came in an array of colours and had a leather flower shaped logo attached to the laces. When Liverpool reached the '81 European Cup Final in Paris I went looking for a different style from what everyone else was wearing. I got quite a plain pair, a totally different style from the norm. It still had the leaf on but on returning to Liverpool I was refused entry to the Harrington, for wearing these Kickers, because they looked like trainees. Sometimes you can try too hard to be different.

The Spring of 1981 saw Kios arrive in an array of bright colours, red, white, blue or lilac. Kickers had certainly led the way as far as wearing loud colours on your feet was concerned. At first, a boot, the 'Rider' was available, fastened with laces. But as soon as Summer arrived, Kios introduced a 'Low' shoe, again fastened with laces.

Someone somewhere soon noticed the fashionable Velcro fastening strap-over trainers that had started to pop up and sure enough, the Kios strap-over appeared. Again Close Encounters had the footwear in first, Neil's Corner on Bold Street also happily took £30 off the young punters or if you popped across to Manchester, Stolen from Ivor had plenty in stock. The shoe is remembered as having the name embossed back to front in bright red letters into the middle of the sole, so that when standing on a muddy path, the imprint would read KIOS correctly.

Jeans & Trainers

The rise and fall in popularity of the jeans and trainers was gaining momentum by the Summer of 1980. Lois had lost face and had been replaced by Inega Drainies or Bib and Brace. On the feet, Forest Hills and also Stan Smith were being scoured for up and down the land.

The market had been saturated with Samba, every kid had a pair and so something more elusive was needed. It was at this time that exclusiveness now meant travelling around the country to find that pair of trainers unavailable in Liverpool. Forest Hills had just been released by adidas and had begun appearing on certain feet but the shops in Liverpool didn't have any. The shoes had been designed in conjunction with NASA and adidas insisted they be supplied only to the top tennis clubs around Britain. White with gold stripes and a white sole, weighing only 250 grammes, they were the lightest tennis shoe in the world, but from where did they appear? Once released to only a few major stores, a bit of detective work was needed. Chris had done some and decided he had to have a pair. 'I hitched down to London as I had heard Lillywhites would have them' Lillywhites on Piccadilly Circus being the largest sports store in Europe. If anywhere had them, it would be here. Established in the Capital in 1863, the store had five floors of all the latest sporting goods. 'I was able to get a pair and I also got a Lonsdale Sweatshirt which wasn't available in Liverpool. That night I bunked the train back to Lime Street. As I walked across the platform, there to my horror was someone with a pair of Forest Hills on. I asked him where he had got them from and he said the Arndale Centre in Manchester. I sold mine the next day without wearing them.' They weren't that elusive after all. The Forest Hills would be re-issued years later with a yellow sole, but only 400 would make it into this Country and Wade Smith purchased the lot for his store.

Chris would make numerous trips to Lillywhites. The sight of many Scousers travelling to the store didn't go un-noticed with the locals and once or twice Chris would have a lucky escape.

Local Boys began hanging around the store on the look out for any unprepared wedge heads. Getting followed around five floors was a bit disconcerting. Similar situations arose for one or two on visits to Manchester's Arndale Centre. Going in a small group could easily draw attention, so it was best to travel in pairs or on your own. Games in London gave many opportunities for visits to Lillywhites and also Dickie Dirts on Fulham Broadway for cheap jeans. Advertising itself as the cheapest in London, the place was obviously worth a visit whenever the Reds were in town. That was until they went bankrupt. Based in a former cinema on Fulham Broadway, the shop was quite pioneering in that it was one of the first to parallel import. Basically, buy the jeans cheaply from a different country and then importing them to the UK without the jean companies consent. They also flouted opening hours laws by opening on a Sunday and trading until 11pm 7 days a week.

Basically the football related hooliganism wasn't just confined to the match. If you looked like you were a Scouser there was always someone who wanted to 'have-a-go'. This included going to Concerts. Travelling outside of Liverpool meant keeping your guard up. One of the most popular groups in these years were The Jam. The Mod revival had gripped many, most teenagers liked the music and that included the football going ones.

On the
29th November 1979,
a £3 ticket got you into
Deeside Leisure Centre.
Gangs from all over
the North West
descended upon Deeside.

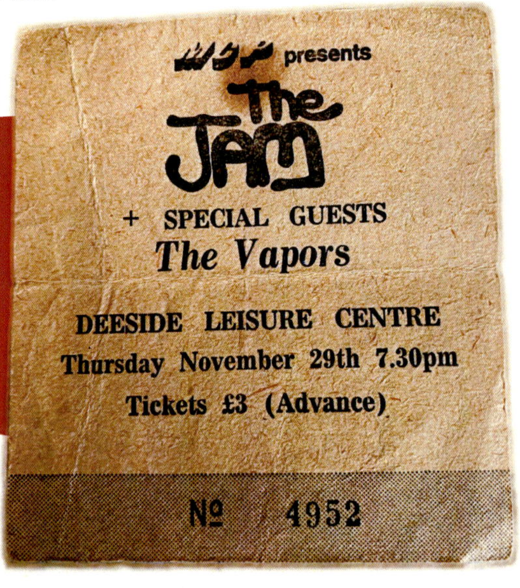

From early evening until late at night, sporadic outbreaks of violence were witnessed in and around the arena. Most involved van loads of Liverpool Mods and Scally's. Being a Mod in '79 was acceptable as its style was quite cool and it was O.K. to go to the match and mix with the new Smoothie Culture that was emerging. By the start of 1980 though many Mods had shed their Parka's and Two-Tone Suits from Gansgear and were getting into baggy jeans and Stan Smiths.

I spent the Summer of 1979 up to Feb 1980 finely attired in Mod gear bought from the likes of 81A which was a vintage second hand shop that had opened in 1977 after re-locating from Birmingham. The shop didn't have a name so everyone called it 81A, as that was it's address on Renshaw Street. There was a bit of history about that destination as it used to be the offices of the 1960s Mersey Beat Newspaper. An early 60s publication about the local music scene that carried many articles and photos of The Beatles before they moved away from Liverpool.

Another gig occasion involved London Mod group Secret Affair playing The Mountford Hall in Liverpool. They had a Cockney following that were making a name for themselves by causing trouble at the groups gigs. They were known collectively as 'The Glory Boys'. Whenever Scousers travelled away there was nearly always going to be trouble. So, a group of Cockneys invading home territory gave cause for concern. As soon as the groups 'Glory Boys' chant went up, no other reason was needed for a bit of a scuffle and the Cockneys were soon being chased out. Even when them 'Nutty Boys' of Madness played at the Empire on Lime Street, word spread that maybe mobs of Cockneys would be appearing and numerous local gangs gathered in close proximity to the Empire. The Two Tone Tour in 1981, also at the Empire, almost ended in a riot.

Virgin

Stan Smith

Stan Smith were an all white classic trainer from adidas that has now sold over 3 million worldwide. This trainer didn't have the stripes like other adidas had. The three stripes were replaced with three rows of perforations in the leather. It was also the first ever all leather trainer. Being worn since the mid 1960s by the tennis stars of the day and known in another incarnation as the Robert Haillet, it would become endorsed by Stan Smith in 1971 after he had won the U.S. Open. His face being printed on the tongue and his name embossed on the heel.

The average trainer price in the UK at this time was £14.99 but the Stan Smiths were sold at the higher end of the price scale for £19.99. Top Man had an adidas concession in-store and Stan Smiths started selling there at six a week. Soon it was twenty a week, then fifty and so on. In the run up to Christmas a phenomenal 2000 pairs were sold. They were the trainer of the year for 1979 and would be worn with pride on match day. Chris paid dearly for having a pair in pristine condition after a night game. Standing at a bus stop with a few Scallys, a kick off started a few yards away. Chris ran over, threw the boot in and hastily retreated back to the bus stop. Seconds later a burly police officer comes over and arrests Chris. Pleading his innocence he enquires how would the officer have known it was him with so many people around. The bizzie replied, it had been his bright white trainers that had given him away. Chris had no answer to that. A hefty fine ensued.

Stan Smith stood out for most of that Winter. They became so common, kids started creating their own designer Stan Smiths by dyeing them. Shades of red, blue or green could be seen on a lot of feet but only a few weeks later flakes of the dye would be peeling off all over the parents living room carpet.

Jeans were now changing by the minute or month. Jesus Bib'n'Brace and Jesus Jeans followed on from the Inega Bib'n'Brace of the previous summer of '79. Alan recalls going to All Mankind on London Road specifically to get the Jesus Bib'n'Brace before Liverpool's away game at Notts Forest in September 1979. Jesus Jeans came and then disappeared into obscurity, but in the 70's, they were more famous for a banned advert that had the message 'He who loves me will follow me.' The guy, Oliviero Toscani, who later on in life also produced the banned Benetton adverts was making a name for himself with his first advertising campaign.

The thing to do was to buy the newest fashion before the next match. The match was now becoming a fashion catwalk. It was the place where people were measured by the cut of their cloth, jeans or trainers. To be asked 'Where d'ya get yer trainees from?' was the ultimate accolade. [Replace 'trainees' with jeans, coat or whatever was the latest trend.] It meant you were up there with the fashion dictators and trendsetters. You knew where to get the most sought after of apparel. Mike had bought a green cycling shirt for the summer but they didn't exactly match his Forest Hills, so he meticulously dyed the trainees bright green to match the top. He lost count the number of times he was asked 'Where d'ya get yer trainees from, Mate?' Young individuals must have been scouring Merseyside for weeks looking for luminous green Forest Hills. Some people didn't bother asking where the trainers were from and stories of kids being mugged for their trainers and Kickers are a sorry truth.

In February 1980, I had just started work as an apprentice Printer in the City Centre on the princely sum of £29 a week. Out went the Second Hand 60s Mod gear. It was time to get back into the local dress scene. Desert Boots were replaced with adidas trainees, I'd still been wearing the latest Jeans but the arl adidas ST2 Cagoule came back out of the Wardrobe to replace the Parka until I'd saved up for a new Jacket. Now it was time to spend my hard earned wages on some of the latest Clobber. I got my first weeks wages on the Friday, cash, no week in hand or money in the bank in them days.

I raced across town to All Mankind to get a pair of Ritzy Baggies. Baggy at the top, and then tapered down to a 16" ankle. If I remember right, a 1" turn-up needed to be added. Baggy jeans had been 'IN' for a week or two, but they had to be matched up with a Stripey. A Stripey being a striped long sleeved Peter Werth Polo T-Shirt, available in a variety of colours but the multi coloured Blue one being the predominant favourite. Wrangler had one out at the time and it wasn't long before the market was flooded with copies. Patches on Lime Street and Richmond Street were one of the first places to get the T-Shirt, but the problem was they sold out as soon as they came in. At £14.99 they were exactly half my weeks wages but you had to have one, so I ran across town every day for about two weeks until they arrived. This seemed to be the norm. Shops sold out as soon as one style took off. Sometimes by the time the shelves were loaded again, the trendsetters had moved on, fashion was moving at such a fast pace, shops were finding it hard to keep up.

Spring/Summer and a lightweight jacket was needed in case of any sudden snowstorms [Bolton]. That ended up being a blouson style Jockey jacket. Green or purple with a white band around the middle, therefore resembling a jockey's silks.

An American influence took a hold for a couple of months in the Summer, with Baseball Tops and Airtex, American Football style T-Shirts, but without the shoulder pads, from the Precinct. These mesh style T-Shirts came in an array of colours and could be matched up with your dyed trainers. Gansgear being one of the favourite shops for most things at this time. Another was Erics on Lime Street. Not related to the club, this shop had been around for quite a few years. Skinheads had ventured there for their Two- Tone kecks and Budgie Jackets, plus it was the only place in the 60's to get your button-down striped Ben Shermans besides Carnaby Street in London. It soon became apparent that Erics were doing quick copies of a few jackets though. The Jockey jacket was soon available at a cheaper price than anywhere else and the same could be said about the Campri ski jacket. A few yards along the road was Tony Harris, a small compact shop like Erics but not as popular during this period.

What was funny at the time was the fact that besides having to look the part, you also had to go to the right shops. You didn't want to be caught walking through town with a Topshop bag for fear of ridicule. Whenever I played football, I made sure the bag I put my dirty boots in was from a good shop. It got that bad that I started getting stick for having designer plastic bags.

By the Winter of 1980 Ski Jumpers began appearing, usually with a few skiers across the chest. Places like Ellis Brigham on Bold Street and other such Winter sports shops like Smith Bayer on Harrington Street stocked expensive Ski Jumpers most of the time but the ones popular were a cheaper version available from most shops. The following year the Ski Jumper would return in a more up-market expensive form when Designer Sportswear became a new phrase.

One shop that had no problem keeping up with the Youth's latest choice of Jeans was the Flemings shop on Walton Road. Flemings Jeans were a Liverpool firm that had been around since the 50s when Teddy Boys were able to go into the store on Scotland Road [before the tunnel was built in 1971] to get their 'drainpipe' or 'stovepipe' jeans custom made. By the time the shop changed location in 1971 it was still being frequented by the Liverpool Youth. This time Skinheads wanted 'Supatuff Jeans' which washed out better than the much darker standard Jeans.

Now the shop was being visited yet again. The jeans had sought favour once more for a couple of months at least. Supatuff were being purchased and bleached on the same day. They would be placed in the sink in a mixture of water and bleach and after an hour or two taken out and rinsed. The result was your own individual pair of bleached denim jeans. The longer they were left in the sink the whiter the jeans became. One thing about Flemings was their stiffness and the ability for the seam to twist around the leg, a bit like the Twisted Levi's from a few years back, although I don't think these were supposed to twist. The early Lois cords done something similar and ended up looking daft.

Flemings even took off in Manchester after a few Mancs had noticed the cutting edge Scousers in an un-heard of [in Manchester] brand. Alan worked for Fiat Knibbs and was often sent to the Manchester branch to work. 'A lad in the Manchester branch asked me to get him a pair of Flemings after seeing mine. He had visited Liverpool City Centre looking for the shop but had gone home empty handed. This gave them the added cachet of being hard to find and so the Mancs were even keener for them. After getting him a pair, it soon snowballed into a little moneyspinner. I must have sold about twenty pairs over the following few weeks. They couldn't believe I could get them for about a tenner although they only cost me £8.'

It looks like Liverpool had given Manchester Flemings. In return, we got F.U.'s. Only available in Manchester's Arndale Centre, carloads of wily Scousers would sneak into enemy territory and return with the Jeans. Speaking in hushed tones so as not to be recognized, the Arndale Centre was inundated every weekend for a couple of months. Many thought the jeans were made in Manchester but they were in fact imported from India and were the first International Jeans Wear Brand launched in India. There's an Urban Myth that one store in Manchester would put the goods purchased by Scousers, into a different coloured bag so that their mates waiting outside could easily identify any Scousers invading Manc Territory.

Between 1978 and 1981, numerous makes of jeans were 'IN' and then 'OUT' within the space of a few weeks of each other. Early on there was Lois, Inega, Jesus, FU's, Second Image, Fruit of the Loom and then such luminaries as Fiorucci, Ritzy, Razzy, Ciao, King, Pace, Lee, Flemings and 051's. 051's being a local Label taking its name from the phone code for the Liverpool area at the time. The styles of the Jeans also changed a bit during the years. Lois drainies, Inega stretch, Ritzy Baggies, Razzy red stitch, King cross cords. Drainies, Baggies or straights. Faded or bleached. Turn-ups or frayed. Cords could be needle, then jumbo, and then crossed. The main criteria was to get a pair before everyone else and make sure they were the right specification, ankle width, one month 16 inch, then with a one-inch turn-up, then frayed, then frayed with a split up the side.

The permutations were endless. Jeanette 'I remember every time my brother bought a pair of jeans in the late 70's, I had to take them apart at the seams and then resow them to make them into skin-tight drainies or 'shit-stoppers' as I called them'

Inspired by a Punk ethos, Skin-Tight Jeans had been at the forefront of the new Culture. Lois, then Inega being at the very start of the movement. Mono got his first pair from the Army and Navy Stores opposite Lewis's 'There wasn't anywhere to get your straight Jeans from except for the Army and Navy Store and they were poor quality, so when Liverpool had their pre-season tour in the Summer of 1977 a few of us were able to get some decent ones from Amsterdam.'

As the transformation from flared Jeans to straight had started, the wearing of the wide legged variety on these early trips to the Continent meant you could slip on a pair of straight jeans in the changing rooms and still get your flares on over the top of them before walking out.

Fiorucci had a store on Hardman Street around 1977 and this would be the first place it was possible to get a pair of drainies. They were quite expensive though as Fiorucci was one of the biggest names in the world of designers at the time.

It wasn't long before 81A on Renshaw Street began stocking second hand 50's and 60's drainpipe Jeans. 81A has become an institution in Liverpool for its endless supply of second hand gear. Changing its position on Renshaw Street in the early 80s to 69A, the store has been frequented by the likes of Mods, Punks, Rockabillies and many others looking for one off pieces of clothing. It is still going strong to this day. Punks would purchase the old second hand gear to de-construct and Mods were able to find fishtail parkas amongst the old army surplus goods on offer.

With Christmas 1980 approaching, cords would be ideal for those Christmas nights out. King Cross Cords in a disgusting red plum colour were snapped up.

They were initially only available from the Arndale Centre in Manchester so an undercover expedition would be taken. Eventually Rocky on Renshaw Street would get them in, just in time for the Christmas rush. Rocky was the sister shop to Giorgio on Mt. Pleasant. Owned by the Goodman family, the firm started out on the Mt. Pleasant site with Harry Gee in the early 70's, then it became Hero's by Harry Gee before eventually changing its name to Giorgio. By the time Giorgio closed its doors for the last time, Rocky had become the designer store of choice for your going-out gear in the early 80s. Importing designer wears from Italy, as anything with 'Made in Italy' on the label would sell in droves. The store even developed its own Italian sounding brand with the Giancarlo Ricci range of clothing.

By Christmas, the Millets Fisherman's Coat was a must have. Blue with yellow on the inside and an over-sized hood. It is possible that these were reversible but they were never worn that way. The Peter Storm Cagoule had been purchased from Millets a couple of years earlier but the Fishermans Coat would be the last time anyone with style paid the shop a visit. Over twenty years later and certain articles of clothing will be fondly remembered. Both of these jackets were classics of the time. Another item on the shopping list for the Christmas party at The Harrington was a Second Image Denim 'Chore' Jacket. Thigh length with big square pockets. Today this style is back in favour and they are known as 'French Chore' Jackets. It was designed and made with a heavy Twill or Denim material to be worn whilst labouring outdoors in France. Its equivalent in the UK was probably the Donkey Jacket.

Coats were now coming and going as quickly as the trainers. If only Ebay had been around in those Shopaholic days. A killing could have been made selling on 'nearly new' clothes every other week.

In the New Year, yet another Jacket arrived that was even more popular. The MA-1 Flight [Bomber] Jacket. A favourite with Cockney Skinheads, especially West Ham's notorious I.C.F. The Jacket was developed in the 1940s for the United States Air Force. A light, high quality nylon but with warm padded insulation.

They came in olive green with an orange inner. The jacket was reversible, so when worn inside out the wearer was noticeable from miles away and could be rescued when in danger. It has never been recorded whether this ever happened at a football match.

The MA-1 was possibly the only piece of apparel that was copied from another team's fans by Scousers during these years. The jacket was a firm favourite with most Cockney clubs. It was advisable to leave the coat at home for games with London teams for fear of being asked the time by your own supporters. Nowhere had the MA-1 in Liverpool, so with getting the N.M.E. every week I noticed it was for sale in the adverts section at the back. I posted off my cheque for £34 including postage and received the jacket a few days later. I told everyone I had travelled to London with my boss on business and was able to get one from Kensington High Street. I didn't want anyone else to be able to get one from the N.M.E. It wasn't until a month or so later that Callans on Manchester Street by the Queensway Tunnel got them in.

Throughout the year of 1980, a keen eye was needed to keep up with the forever-changing wardrobe of Jackets, Jeans and Trainers. After Stan Smith had been blunted by familiarity, a few different names were given a run. Obviously, they had to be hard to get hold of. Brooks [an American company] were worn by Jimmy Connors at Wimbledon and weren't dissimilar to Stan Smith being all white but with the initials JC in blue on the side. Eric travelled to Southport to get a pair and didn't tell anyone for months where he had got them from.

The Italians also got in on the act with the Diadora Borg Elite which had uppers made of the finest kangaroo leather, and with the Bjorn Borg signature on the side. This year was definitely the start of a Tennis influence in firstly the footwear with the Stan Smith's and then eventually the overall look.

Bjorn Borg had dominated Men's Tennis in the late 70's, culminating in a fifth Wimbledon Title in 1980, each time wearing a pair of Diadora Elite. In 1978, Diadora added his name to the shoe and they would eventually become a sought after classic.

1980 had seen many a keen-eyed Scouser tuning into T.V. coverage of Wimbledon, not necessarily for the Tennis but mainly to cast an eye on the Labels being sported by the likes of Borg, Jimmy Connors and John McEnroe etc. Come the end of the Summer names such as Fila, Sergio Tacchini, Cerruti 1881 and even Nike [which wasn't a household name as yet] were implanted into the minds of many a design hungry Scouser.

European Travel

Liverpool have always had a reputation for being the best scam artists in the country. It wasn't long before many European Cities were being put to the test. For many years those fans had been escaping to the Continent and many a City have had their Shops security put to the test, although security did not seem to be the operative word in many places.

Terry was still at School but managed to get over to Bruges in Belgium for the 1976 UEFA Cup Final. He still remembers Scallys entering the pub he was in with stolen leather box jackets. Very Bryan Ferry at the time.

During the following season, the travelling fans began to be more fashion conscious. The game in St Etienne France is remembered for Sunny Climes and the locals being dressed in some fine attire. Pastel coloured T-Shirts, Shorts, Yachting Pumps, a look that would sneak into the Scouse wardrobe in the following few years. After the glory that was Rome, the flags, banners, scarves, flares [the Jeans variety, not the pyro type] were to be put to rest. Preseason 1977 and the Amsterdam Tournament was an ideal opportunity to wear those flares for the last time and put them to good use by putting on a pair of straights underneath, before walking out of the Shop.

A Second European Cup was added at the end of the 1977/78 season but the following Year saw an early departure from the tournament thanks to Nottingham Forest, although a Super Cup game in Anderlecht enabled some more Duty Free shopping. Yet again another early exit with Dinamo Tblisi followed in 1979/80. Finally in 1981 the Reds were to gain a third European Title in Paris and so more excursions abroad for reasons other than the match could be had.

By now the happening fashions on Merseyside had taken on a new twist. adidas still held the crown in the footwear stakes but a new style was being sported by the select few. They had obviously been acquired from abroad, narrowed down on further enquiry to Germany. Liverpool had been in Stuttgart on preseason duty in the August of 1980 and so this specific shoe had certainly caught the eye.

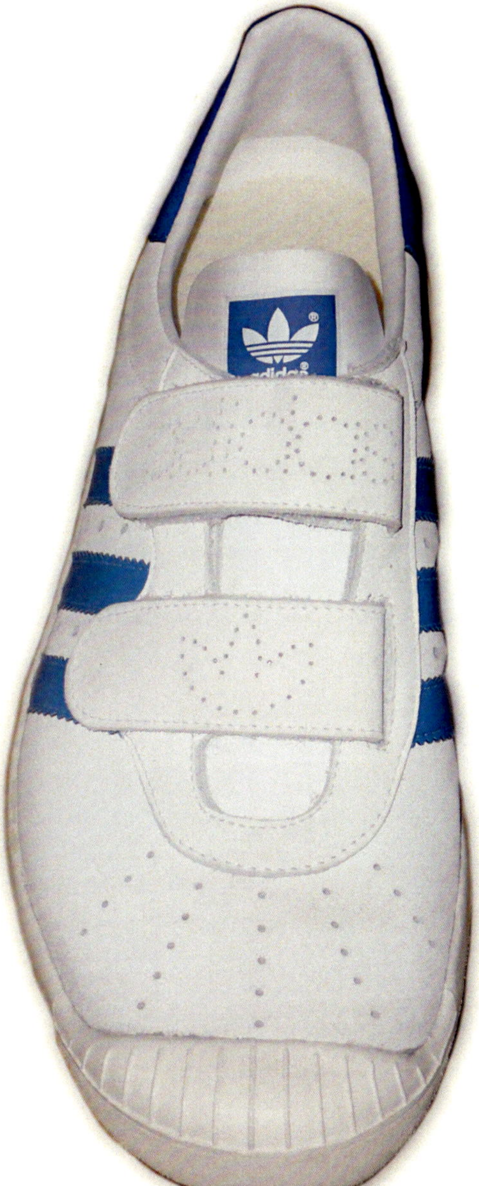

These adidas weren't your usual laced variety of trainer though, they were fastened with two Velcro straps and were white with blue stripes. One strap had adidas spelt in perforations while the other had the trefoil logo on. Their originality had shops in Liverpool inundated with requests for strap-over trainers. As the adidas Tennis Comfort trainer was that elusive other Velcro strap-overs would suffice.

During the Winter of 1980 other makes became available and were duly purchased if the adidas were unobtainable. Donnay became popular, another was the Patrick Ocean and a Le Coq Sportif pair, plus the originators of the strap-over in 1969 Puma came up with the Davis Cup. An all white trainer with the words Davis Cup in gold foil [print] on the straps.

Tony went to Whitty's on School Lane and came out empty handed after the owner told him 'Why would I get a Summer tennis shoe in store to sell in the Winter?' Surely the guy would see reason in the next few weeks after more and more requests for the adidas or Donnay strap-over were heard. Eric 'Every Friday for about four weeks I went to Jack Sharps and Heslop and Duckinfield and got told they would be in the following week. Eventually I got a pair but they were possibly the worst trainers to have in winter because of the flat sole with not much grip. As soon as it rained you ended up on your arse'. This, almost certainly, was due to the shoes being a Summer Tennis trainer. Pretty soon, the adidas Tennis Comfort and the Donnay arrived in Town on the same day. With working in the City Centre I had been trying, day after day, to get a pair for myself and two mates. One Wednesday before a Liverpool night game, I was able to get two adidas and a pair of Donnay in time for the match. Alan recalls that night, 'I remember walking through the car park under the Main Stand and the three of us had these brand new, gleaming white strap-overs on.

Everyone was staring at our feet and one or two asked us where we got them from.' To have the shoes the day of the game meant not many would have them that night. It gave a feeling of personal pride. The match was the place to be seen and to turn up in something everyone was after was a great feeling. A tip was to scuff and dirty the trainers after buying them, so people would think they were a few months old.

Having something new, whether it was the trainers or new clothes, gave a certain feeling of pride and confidence. John recalls 'Around these years I wasn't working and was always skint. I'd have enough money for a night out and I'd go to meet the mate at his house. He would have half a dozen Designer shirts hanging up that his ma had ironed and would be trying each one on, in front of the mirror. I used to borrow one that he wasn't going to wear. When we went out it was as though I was a different person. I was so confident and would be chatting up all the birds, thinking how great I looked, just because I had this Designer shirt on.'

The most noticeable fact about the adidas Comfort and its part in Casual History, is that it is probably the first trainer acquired from Europe that was un-available in the UK. So what this now meant was that to keep up with this ever-changing fashion of footwear, you had to travel abroad. Liverpool's European games, whether Summer friendlies or European Cup games, gave ample opportunity for many 'Straights/Smoothies' to get their hands on the most elusive of trainers and Designer wear. Many black marketeers sprang up overnight and some would make a decent living, making cheap trips abroad to stock up on the latest Sportswear. It wasn't only friends or family that were clamouring for the goods but many clothes stores such as Wade Smith were also willing to pay for the gear knowing that there would be a good mark up in price for them, such was the demand.

During the 1970s the travelling supporter had to put up with the travel arrangements selected by their Clubs, expensive Flights or arduous Coach journeys. Coach firms such as Lawrensons and Towns Travel did the European trips but didn't offer the comfort or speed of a train. By the end of the decade though the train would take the strain.

Transalpino

In a small row of shops next to a butchers, nestled a Mecca for many a would be traveller. Close to Paddys Wigwam [Metropolitan Cathedral] the Transalpino shop on Myrtle Parade became a godsend for Liverpool supporters travelling to Europe between the years of 1978 and 1985. Offering Student Rail Travel at a very competitive price compared to the airlines and Coaches, the shop sold tickets to anyone under the age of 26.

On opening in 1978, the next door Butcher advised on fitting steel shutters to the shop front. This was duly done, although it did not stop the safe being taken on one occasion.

Transalpino was a British Company owned by the Janonne family. Set up in the 1950s to shift migrant workers around Europe, the company came into it's own in an 80s era associated with the Casuals predilection for European travel. Italian Toni Brandi got things up and running on Londons Shaftesbury Avenue with a first floor office and a tiny shop. Victoria Station soon followed. In all, ten branches throughout the British Isles eventually opened, four in London [Victoria Station, Shaftesbury Avenue and two on Buckingham Palace Road, plus one in Edinburgh, Glasgow, Dublin, Belfast, Birmingham and Liverpool. The company also sold tickets through all University student travel offices and a few high street agents.

It's a fair assumption to say the Liverpool Branch did very well in these formative years, from the exodus of supporters, even taking into account the loss of a safe plus the fact that no-one seemed to travel further than Ostend or Calais. As Liverpool F.C. went about their business collecting European trophies, Transalpino's clientele grew, as word spread, not only about the cheap rail travel but also about the scam of doctoring the tickets.

SUMMER 82
FROM MAY 23

TRANSALPINO
BIGE

Authorised trains
Treni autorizzati
Trains autorises
Toegelaten trainen

TT14

THIS TIMETABLE MUST NOT BE REMOVED FROM COVER

SUBJECT TO ALTERATION FROM SEPTEMBER 26TH

R	R		R		RS				RS					
0928			1328				Dep LONDON VICTORIA Arr			0715				1948r)
	0940f)				1940		Dep LONDON LIVERPOOL ST Arr		0914b)				1923	
	1115				2145		Dep HARWICH PARKESTON Q Arr		0645				1715	
							Dep FOLKESTONE HARBOUR Arr			0445				
1140			1530				Dep DOVER WESTERN DOCKS Arr							1740
1213	317		219		407		----TRAIN NUMBERS----------		406	1432			316	1212 / 244
N			N		0715		Dep HOEK VAN HOLLAND Arr		2213				1053	
1730	1930		2115				Dep OOSTENDE Arr			0055				1303
2227			0146				Arr KOLN HBF Dep			2050				0735
	2214				0956		Arr MONCHENGLADBACH HBF Dep		1918				0753	
2837	3565	3081	2843/ 453 T	453	5419	2747	----TRAIN NUMBERS----------	3178	2746	2842/ 452 T	452	3172	5114	3104
	2228	2243		0953	1024	1315	Dep MONCHENGLADBACH HBF Arr	1849	1703		1940	0743	0736	
2345			1009				Dep KOLN HBF Arr			1930				0711
	2302				1057	1336	Arr DUSSELDORF HBF Dep	1818				0709		
		2322		1025	1129u)	1353	Arr DUISBURG HBF Dep		1628		1906		0644	
		2353		1053d)	1155u)		Arr OBERHAUSEN HBF Dep		1617d)		1827d)		0635v)	
		0018d)		1041		1417	Arr ESSEN HBF Dep		1611		1848		0615d)	
		0035d)		1053		1429	Arr BOCHUM HBF Dep		1557		1836		0602d)	
		0012		1120e)	1156u)		Arr GELSENKIRCHEN HBF Dep		1602d)		1809d)		0612v)	
		0040		1108		1447	Arr DORTMUND HBF Dep		1543		1823		0545v)	
0019	0015		1047		1146		Arr WUPPERTAL-ELBERFELD Dep	1738		1849		0644		0627
0045	0059		1108		1229		Arr HAGEN HBF Dep	1713		1829		0618		0557
		0113		1128		1511	Arr HAMM (WESTF) Dep		1520		1802			
			1155	1159		1534	Arr SOEST Dep		1454	1746	1738			
			→	1240		1614	Arr PADERBORN Dep		1413	←	1703			
				1254		1627	Arr ALTENBEKEN Dep		1401		1649			
				1325		1653	Arr WARBURG Dep		1337		1624			
				1359		1728	Arr KASSEL Dep		1302		1549			
				1533k)		1833k)	Arr GOTTINGEN Dep		1151k)		1421k)			
				1454			Arr BEBRA Dep				1458			
				1756			Arr ERFURT Dep				1210			
				1940			Arr LEIPZIG HBF Dep				1030			
				2145z)			Arr KARL-MARX-STADT Dep				0640z)			
				2144z)			Arr DRESDEN HBF Dep				0818z)			

N Reservation recommended
R Reservation obligatory
S Supplement payable
T Through coaches to/from Leipzig

b) Arr 0905 on Sundays
d) Change at Duisburg Hbf
e) Change at Essen Hbf
f) Dep 20 mins earlier on Sundays
k) Change at Kassel
r) Slightly later on Sundays
u) Change at Dusseldorf Hbf
v) Mons to Fris only
z) Change at Leipzig Hbf

ALL TRAINS EXCEPT T.E.E. ARE AUTHORISED IN THE NETHERLANDS
ALL TRAINS EXCEPT T.E.E. ARE AUTHORISED IN BELGIUM
ALL TRAINS EXCEPT T.E.E. ARE AUTHORISED BETWEEN AACHEN & KOLN
FOR FULL DETAILS OF LONDON-KOLN SERVICE SEE TT3 & TT4
TICKETS ROUTED VIA OOSTENDE ARE NOT VALID VIA HOEK VAN HOLLAND & VICE VERSA
PASSENGERS ARE ADVISED TO MAKE PRIOR RESERVATIONS
PASSENGERS ARE STRONGLY URGED TO CHECK ALL TIMES LOCALLY

SEE REVERSE FOR IMPORTANT PASSENGER INFORMATION

The 'Tranalpino Rub-Out' became synonymous with the era and was a truly innovative way of saving money for many a Scouser whose giro would not stretch as far as Germany or Switzerland. Paying for a ticket to Ostend and then altering the final destination or in some cases just writing the destination on the carbon copy of the ticket, more often than not guaranteed arrival at the City of choice. In the early years the destinations would be written in pencil by the shop staff, would you believe? Pure Scouse bravado and cheek, plus the language barrier, may also have played its part.

As the 80s unfolded, Europe beckoned. An appetite for new training shoes and Designer Sportswear took a hold. The Transalpino logo during this period became as recognisable as any Fila or Tacchini badge. Football supporters and fans of fashion caught the zeitgeist easily, trekking across uncharted territory to see nights of European glory and liberate Sports Shops of their epochal brands.

The English Sun set on European football in 1985 and it was as though Transalpino had also run its course. In-house fighting and some National Companies pulling in debts brought to an end a Company without whom the last great revolution in men's clothing may not have happened. All the U.K. shops closed at the same time and Company Director Aldo Janonne retired to Poland to become a pig farmer. The U.K. and its band of travelling Casuals had lost one of its main protagonists.

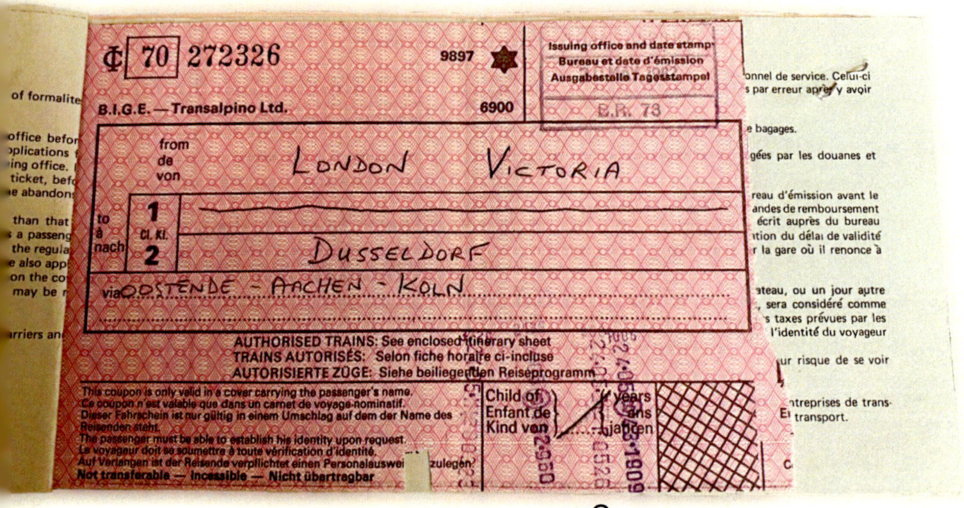

Munich '81 - Tales Of Trains To Far Flung Places

April 1981 and Liverpool get the draw every trainer hungry wag wanted, A team from West Germany [Home of adidas]. Bayern Munich in the European Cup. £52.95 by Transalpino, if you paid the full fare plus 20 deutschmarks [£5] for the match ticket. Now was the time to kill two birds with one stone, See Liverpool through to the European Cup Final [although a 0-0 at Anfield kept the tie finely balanced] and capture the latest pair of adidas unavailable back home.

Liverpool played their part, Ray Kennedy scoring their goal in a 1-1 draw enabling Liverpool to progress to the Final in Paris. The adidas Grand Prix launched in 1970 and its sleek design captured the hearts of many Tennis Pro's. Worn by Ilie Nastase, they had double density PU man made soles and were known for their comfort. These were then to be the trainer of choice. Another adidas trainer others thought interesting was the Trimm-Trab. Though the bright colours may have put some off, a few would return with them. Most trainers over the last three years had been white except for the Samba. Within months the Trimm-Trab were a must have and many regretted not getting them on this trip.

Peter remembers being in a Sports Shop on the Rheinplatz in Munich. 'We were just looking at the trainers when a group of lads came in. One started chatting to the bird by the till while his mates began trying on new Grand Prix and Wimbledon. Thing was, the trainers were displayed in pairs, not just single ones on show like in the U.K. By the time these lads left they all had new trainers on and their old ones were left on the shelf in the store.' Many months later, the Grand Prix and the adidas Wimbledon hit these shores, with their price being a whopping £29.99, but apparently only in Liverpool.

While still working in Top Man, Wade Smith had managed to convince his adidas bosses to import the Wimbledon trainer. Five hundred pairs landed. Made in Austria with the adidas name and logo on the middle stripe. Later versions without the name and logo and Made in Yugoslavia would be shunned on Merseyside because of this. Insistence on the finer details was the ultimate factor.

Cigarettes were aplenty in Germany. Cigarette machines were spread across the towns on street corners. A packet of 20 cost three Deutschmarks [75p] but the Deutschmark was exactly the same size as our very own 5p piece. Therefore, a packet of Marlboro or any other well known brand cost those in the know 15p. This little scam was probably the forerunner for many cigarette runs in later years. There was always some way of making money on these Awaydays and it didn't matter how, so long as some money was recouped to pay for the trip. Besides getting the ciggies in Munich, I thought another nice little moneymaker would be the Match Day programme. The sellers nearly always got done (robbed) and this trip was no exception. I had about five rolled up in my coat pocket and as the final whistle went a good few of us were up, over the moat, and onto the pitch to congratulate our heroes. As I sped across the pitch, the programmes slipped out of my pocket. Dilemma! I had to get the programmes. They would fetch good money back at the Programme shop by the Kop or the numerous programme fairs around at the time. Suddenly as I stopped to get them, a member of the local Polizei jumps on me. Next thing is, I'm being escorted out of the Ground and luckily for me I'm just left outside. Good job them Munich fans weren't into the hooligan thing at the time, with me being alone. I walked around the Ground back to our end and met the mates before we were off to the Bierkeller for a few Steins to celebrate.

Liverpool were now into another European Final. This one in the French capital of Paris. Yet another chance to sample some European hospitality. Paris may well be one of the fashion capitals of the world but when it came to adidas trainers, it was probably on par with Birkenhead. The shopkeepers on the Champs Elysee though probably couldn't believe the so-called English hooligans pleasantly strolling down the Boulevards looking for Sports Shops and even an imaginary adidas Centre. One Shop paid a visit to see what new designs were to be had was the Kickers store. There wasn't much to show from the visit to Paris, but in those days there was no break before an England game and two days after the European Cup Final England played in Basel against Switzerland in a World Cup Qualifier. About twelve of us were staying in Paris for the week, so we all decided to use our extendable Transalpino tickets to travel down to Basel on the Thursday over-night train. Basel was ideally placed on the border with Germany, so what other reason would be needed to show a bit of patriotism. We arrived early Friday morning and checked into a hotel. Then it was a short 20 minute walk across the border to find the nearest Sports Shop.

I remember the adidas Grand Slam looked a bit different. A lot of money had obviously gone into the design process. Different coloured shock absorbers through the heel. Three red, white and blue pegs were included for each shoe. You could then put in whichever coloured pegs felt the more comfortable or helped you run faster should the need arise. I remember having to pay £35 for them, which was an extortionate amount in them days. A weeks wages for me at the time. Every time I arrived home with a new purchase, my arl fella's favourite saying would be heard, 'How much? I could buy a car for that!'. adidas were trying out the 'peg system' in a couple of different style trainers including the L.A. and Keglers. The Grand Slam looked the best though. A key peg removal tool was included in the purchase to be able to remove and replace the pegs. The pegs were supposed to help with the comfort and suspension, therefore helping you perform better on the Tennis Court. The Grand Slam only lasted a few months before the heel wore away where the pegs went through.

Eric was on the same trip and returned with an extremely cheap pair of Grand Prix. 'We were in a German Sports Shop and I asked if I could pay in Francs meaning French Francs [left over from Paris], the woman thought I meant Swiss Francs and asked for 25 Francs. After paying her in French Francs, we made a sharp exit. The cost worked out at about £2.50. We disappeared hastily back across the border.'

Now, if trips to the Arndale Centre or Lilywhites were a bit hazardous, a venture to watch an England game in the early 80's could have been life threatening for Scousers. We arrived in Basle on the day of the Match. Apparently, there had been trouble the previous night with the local Italian Community. England fans sought revenge on the night of the game. We thought it best to keep ourselves to ourselves, so a bit of Shopping was done and then a few quiet drinks before making our way to the ground. Things couldn't have worked out better as we were able to bunk into the Main Stand, which was occupied by members of the England Supporters Club who seemed quite a decent bunch. Anyway, you don't get many local Italians going to watch Switzerland versus England and the Swiss were still quite gentile, so all of these pent-up hooligans in the England end start knocking ten tons of shite out of each other. It seemed to last most of the game and ended up being better viewing than the England team who got beat 2-1. Liverpool's Terry McDermott scoring the consolation goal. After the game about 5,000 Swiss bikes got destroyed by the rampaging mob. Anyway we made it safely home after a fantastic week watching Liverpool lift another European Cup and I didn't have to use the go-faster pegs in my new Grand Slam at the England match.

Liverpools Pre-Season Tour in the Summer of 1981 gave the chance for some to stock up on more trainers after the disappointment that was Paris. Three Games in Switzerland against Zurich, Geneva and Neuchatel Xamax gave many opportunities for the acquisition of Grand Prix, Wimbledon, Grand Slam and the newest addition Trimm-Trab. It also became apparent that these sleepy Swiss towns were quite un-prepared for any invasions and so many shops were duly liberated of their clothing, trainers and even jewellery. The word 'shoplifting' did not seem to appear in the Swiss dictionary.

Whilst Liverpool fans were traipsing around sports shops all over Europe in 1981, the Top Man store in Liverpool was busying itself selling any new adidas it could get it hands on. 7,000 pairs of classic German footwear were flying off the shelves. The Leisure Walking Shoe range of Palermo, Korsica and the Tenerife Slip Ons came and went in the course of one year. Robert Wade-Smith was checking National Statistics for these shoes as he couldn't believe the sales. Robert 'I was looking at the National numbers, 90% in Liverpool, 9% in Manchester and 1% in the rest of the UK ! Once I opened Wade Smith on Slater Street in the November of 1982 that fad had run its course. All Schools banned them for a start but also adidas Germany ceased production too.'

The clothes this year now went up-market. Anything that was 'Made in Italy' seemed to be on the most wanted list. Fila, Ellesse, Robe di Kappa and Sergio Tacchini were all Italian brands but Liverpool City Centre didn't have much on offer in the way of this new Designer Sportswear and so trips abroad offered the best chance to get the new gear. Italian made Sabre Jumpers from Issy Crown seemed to be the only worthwhile purchase.

Fila had become a household name to many who knew their labels. It was Bjorn Borgs exploits over the years that had brought the name 'Fila' to everyone's attention. I travelled to Amsterdam for Liverpool's European Cup game with A.Z. Alkmaar 67 in October of '81. We stayed for a couple of nights and so could scour the City for the best in Sportswear. The main Department Store, De Bijenkorf, had a whole floor dedicated to all the latest names. After trying on a navy blue Fila Ski jumper in the changing rooms, the coat went on over it and it was time to leave. The mate Eric did the same.

The whole rack of jumpers had no alarm tags and so a quick exit was had. It was too good an opportunity to miss. There was a bit of a scare on the way out though, a big security guard next to alarm barriers by the exit. We had to go to the bogs just make sure there were no tags on the jumpers. It was only on leaving the bogs that we noticed alarm barriers by the toilets as well. We had walked through them going into the toilets. We knew then we were O.K. Outside, the mate and I bumped into four lads we knew from the away games. On telling them of our exploits, they headed off towards the Department Store. The next time we saw them was on the ferry back to Dover, they had cleared the whole rack of about 20 Ski jumpers. We also found a nice little Sports Shop down a side street where I was able to purchase an adidas Lendl Jumper with the diamond chest and convinced the shop assistant to give me a boss Fila Bjorn Borg Point of Sale advert.

European stores weren't used to such blasé antics as walking into a store and filling up a Head Bag and walking out. Many didn't have the clothes tagged and the training shoes were usually found in pairs making them a lot easier to lift. A few years earlier on a pre-season tour, a group of lads visited a massive Fiorucci store for days on end, filling up sports bags and eventually having to send some of the stuff home by air, they had that much. After filling up the bags, they just walked out. 'He wears the finest clothes / the best designers heaven knows..... Halston, Gucci, Fiorucci.' So sang Sister Sledge in 1979 and these lads had an eye for the quality and style that put Fiorucci up there with Gucci.

These types of firms were cutting their teeth in the world of thieving as they followed Liverpool throughout Europe. Back home, there were many customers only too willing to pay a good price for the goods. Within a year, it became obvious which countries were more lapse in security. Certain towns on the outskirts of major Cities in Germany and places in Switzerland became destinations for professional theft and card fraud.

Even if there wasn't a game on the Continent, many trips were made. Paul 'Some lads we knew had done a couple of trips, so, we decided to have a go. We did the Transalpino rub-out and headed for West Germany. After the first visit we realised the quiet towns just outside of the major Cities were the least security conscious. Looking back, there wasn't a lot you could bring back in a sports bag. A couple of jumpers, a half dozen T-Shirts and about four pairs of trainers, plus you would wear the coat and a few other bits. The best stuff you would wear at the weekend and then sell it as new during the week. If you remember, the top Italian Sportswear wasn't cheap, even in Germany, but we still made a decent profit because it didn't cost us anything in the first place.'

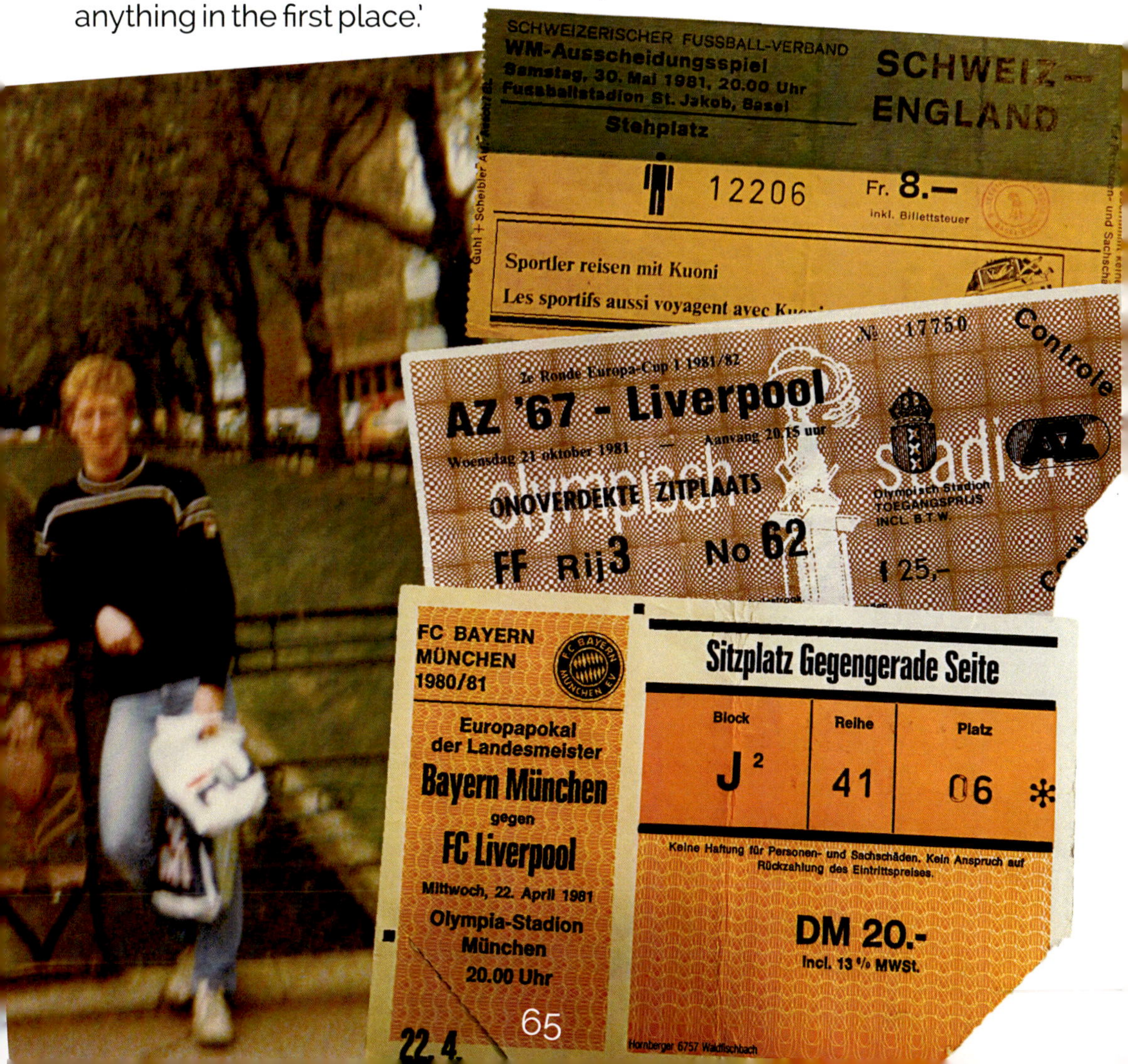

Skullduggery

Unemployment in 1980 hit the 2 million figure for the first time since the 1930s and Liverpool would be one of the hardest hit regions in the country. If you wanted to keep up with what was going on in the world of fashion on Merseyside you needed to have a job [if you were one of the lucky ones] or you had to beg, steal or borrow. These kids, who didn't realise they were creating a new sub-culture, had grown up in the hard times of the 1970's. During this period on Merseyside, it seemed that your dad was always on strike. The Dockers and Fords had plenty of time out, also there was a three-day week, which affected everyone, power cuts sitting with candles, plus numerous other strikes. It was no wonder that the older teenagers grew up wanting that bit more. Those lucky enough to leave school and gain an apprenticeship happily spent their cash on the latest fashion. As long as you could afford the clothes, the match and a few pints at the weekend everything was good. Being Liverpool, those who didn't work still wanted the same things and so quite a bit of skulduggery took place.

In 1979, Liverpool and Everton fans started making the pages of all the daily papers. Those getting the Ordinary to away games were finding themselves with a bit of free time to wander around City Centres. Within a two-month period five high profile incidents occurred, each making the pages of the Echo. Feb; There was a report of 'Fagin' type gangs going to Liverpool away games to pickpocket home fans after 27 victims at the Southend F.A. Cup game. This happened even though Merseyside Police had tipped off Southend C.I.D. but no arrests were made.

March 10:
Liverpool fans rampage at Ipswich robbing a Mens Clothing Store.

April 24:
39 arrests at Notts Forest v Liverpool game after a running battle between 1000 fans. On the train journey home the communication cord is pulled at Uttoxeter. The town is invaded and a jewellers is robbed of a £15,000 haul.

May 1:
Bolton v Liverpool Up to 300 Liverpool fans rampage through Bolton City Centre raiding 8 shops for cash and goods. The haul is £1000 worth.

May 5:
Tottenham v Everton 100 fans run rampage along Pentonville Road near Kings Cross smashing a jewellers window and stealing thousands of pounds worth of jewellery. Liverpool's executive liaison officer Jim Kennefick needed to speak out over the incidents. He accused the gangs of hooligans and thieves of ruining Liverpools name by posing as supporters. Hooliganism had become a National obsession and every club had an unruly element. While many supporters of other clubs were attempting to out-fight each other, those on Merseyside always seemed to have an ulterior motive for running amok.

Wade Smith

The latest adidas styles available in West Germany were expensive and was one reason why they weren't introduced here by the U.K Stores. A lot more technology was being used to produce the designs and this was pushing up the price. It was only the foresight of a certain Robert Wade-Smith, who knew that the kids in Liverpool were only too willing to pay any amount to have the best, that more trainers would cross the Channel. When the travelling Liverpool fans arrived home with their new adidas, 50,000 kids on Merseyside would want these new highly desirable styles. By the end of 1982, Robert had opened up his own store on Slater Street selling mainly adidas.

Robert Wade-Smith started out in 1977 working for a Yorkshire Company called Peter Black who had won the rights to produce adidas bags. 2 or 3 million bags were being produced each year and because of this success Peter Blacks was offered the distribution of adidas sportswear throughout the U.K. Robert tells us of his early years 'I learnt the business initially in the Factories. Then I went to the adidas Warehouses the following year, for a year. My own personal story goes back to the Autumn of 1977 when I was apprenticed in a job on the Factory floor where I was cording the iconic adidas 1708 and 1960 bag handles for 4 months and then riveting the steel studs into bases of the also famous flight-bags for some time too. Then a further 6 months as a 'floor-boy' sweeper and raw materials go-fer too! Plus a year of 'down the Mill' hard-labour followed by another year of lugging 10's of thousands of adidas cartons in the dustiest of an old Velvet Mill. Millions of Goods-in and Goods-out! It was ghastly in that Warehouse. The Factory floor taught me everything one ever really needs to know about both 'time & motion' slick productivity but more importantly how the craft and love of making things was lost in big scale production line manufacturing. How the smaller and more TLC/intimate way of making say Mulberry handbags was much more akin to the love of artisanship. Especially at the home~working level too.

But my tough apprenticeship was the price to pay just to get on the subsequent management training program. Where, I must admit, I was then fast-tracked through many sales and especially retail relevant experiences. Then they put me on a sales course, after which I was then put onto the adidas concessions business. That was the adidas shop business which had 20 concessions around the UK in Top Man stores. I was the guy despatched every Friday morning during the Autumn of 1979 to drive the 100 pairs a week of Stan Smith's to Liverpool (Top Man Church Street, where we had a concession shop-inshop), to fuel the remarkable origins of what would become the '80s Casuals Movement'.

In the Winter of 1980, Robert attempted to get adidas distributors to supply the Forest Hills Trainer to the adidas concession store in Liverpool. 500 pairs had arrived in the Country for distribution but had sat in a Warehouse for nearly a year. Eventually receiving just 10 pair, they went on sale in October 1980 at the princely sum of £39.99. Within days, they were sold. Robert had confirmed the theory to his bosses, that the punters on Merseyside were willing to pay for a rare, exclusive shoe. Now for the remainder. Robert received the other shoes in the run-up to Christmas. They had Sold Out by Christmas Eve. The store in Top Man Liverpool was selling three times the amount of adidas than any other concession around the Country. Robert confirms 'I saw this phenomenal opportunity in Liverpool, it was a micro market, unreal really. It wasn't happening anywhere else in the Country or even the World, the way it was in Liverpool. The average price of adidas trainers in the UK was £17 at the time whilst in Liverpool it was £30.' The Forest Hills had poured scorn on the fact that the UK market could not sell a £30/£35 trainer.

Robert was involved in controlling those 20 concession stores and drove around the UK for three years. For those 150+ weeks not only was Liverpool number one in sales every week, but out of the twenty shops, they were also triple the sales of the second placed store. In fact they were doing a third of the total business adidas did in the U.K.

Soon he was looking for Special Imports for the Liverpool Store from the German, French and Austrian factories. Before opening his own place, he succeeded in acquiring Wimbledon and Grand Prix. The range of styles expanded in the Top Man store from twenty to forty or fifty.

Interestingly, adidas were nervous selling running shoes to Top Man. They thought it might damage their reputation and undo their heritage for Sport. The shop was supposed to be selling an adidas leisure range including Samba but there was no stopping the boom. The cult for training shoes would see people in Liverpool owning 2 or 3 pairs against the National average of less than one pair.

Robert wasn't from Liverpool but having always wanted to open his own shop there could be no other place to start. 'The fact that the trainer boom was happening around me was just opportunism from my point of view. Anybody else with some entrepreneurism or flair, had they had my job, would have done the same because where else in the world would you start it other than in Liverpool? So I packed my bags and moved to Liverpool. Angie, now my wife, but my girlfriend at the time, moved over with me and we literally set up the backstreet shop on Slater Street. We started with £500 and lived in a bedsit for the first six months of our lives.'

The opening of the Wade Smith store on Slater Street more or less put paid to the travelling abroad for just trainers. From now on, the newest trainers were available from the shop on Slater Street with the giant adidas Marathon trainer in the window. Robert 'I had just turned 22 when I walked out of adidas' offices with just £500 to my name. But my gleaned 'insights' were to be worth millions already. That back-street shop in Liverpool beckoned. As a Private Boarding School, middle class, countryside young guy, it felt like emigrating to Moscow. However my powers of persuasion and motivational skills were also invaluable to set me on my 'Pedlars Journey'!'

At £1500 a year rent, it was possible to sell just three pairs of trainers a week to keep the store open. It wasn't the best of starts though, as on arriving on the first day of trading, 1st November 1982, those big white doors are opened to the sight of a major break-in with 70% of the stock missing. What could have had a devastating effect on morale eventually made Robert even more determined to succeed. Things couldn't get any worse. Robert 'There was about 30 or 40 burnt out matches on the floor in a pile, so these lads that had broken in were trying to find more stock around my stock room. It was a bit of an amateur job but it was pretty soul destroying for me. Fortunately my insurance with Norwich Union was unbelievable. I paid the £125 premium on the Friday and I was ringing them up on the Monday with most of my stock gone. I think it was a couple of thousand pounds worth of stock that I hadn't even paid for from adidas that had been stolen. And Norwich Union paid that £2000 back about ten days later. In fact my bank rang me up to say I've had a good day. They said, "What's this £2000 that's landed in your bank account?" I said, "No, it's the insurance claim". The bank was getting excited because they thought that I was having a good trading time.'

The last great trainer of 1981, brought back from abroad that was still unavailable in the UK was the adidas Trimm-Trab. A running shoe with an indented polyurethane sole that became an icon of Terrace Casuals up and down the land. Available in many different shades and colours Paul was made up to purchase a rare black and white pair from someone returning from a trip abroad. The trainers were added to the German fitness range 'Trimm Dich' that had been around since 1976. The Collection included clothing with a footprint logo instead of the adidas trefoil positioned on the chest.

They had become the 'must have' shoe of 1981-83. Robert Wade-Smith had noticed many lads wearing Trimm-Trab in his first week of opening the store. His takings in that first week had amounted to a paltry £41, and then £110 in the second. This obviously had something to do with his stock. He began enquiries as to where the Trimm-Trab had been purchased. He was told they were from Brussels.

Little did he know this was a ruse and the lads weren't going to give away their little secret. He decided to shut up shop and pay the place a visit, hoping to make a large purchase for his store. Brussels though had nothing to offer but there would be a twist of fate on the journey home. Robert bumps into a few experienced travellers in a Café while awaiting the ferry in Ostend. On telling them of his newly opened shop, he enquires if they had any trainers to sell. The lads seemed un-interested but to Roberts delight they appear on the train from Euston and show him their haul. As well as Ellesse and Lacoste clothes, they had Trimm-Trab in many colours plus Munchen and Grand Slam trainers. On offering to buy them there and then, the lads refuse but the following day they turn up at Slater Street with their Head Bags and 25 pairs of assorted Trainers. Robert is able to haggle them down to £16 a pair. Within 10 minutes of the shop opening he had sold half a dozen pairs at £34.99 each. By closing time only two pair remained. This was to be the most magical day in Roberts and the Wade Smith store's history.

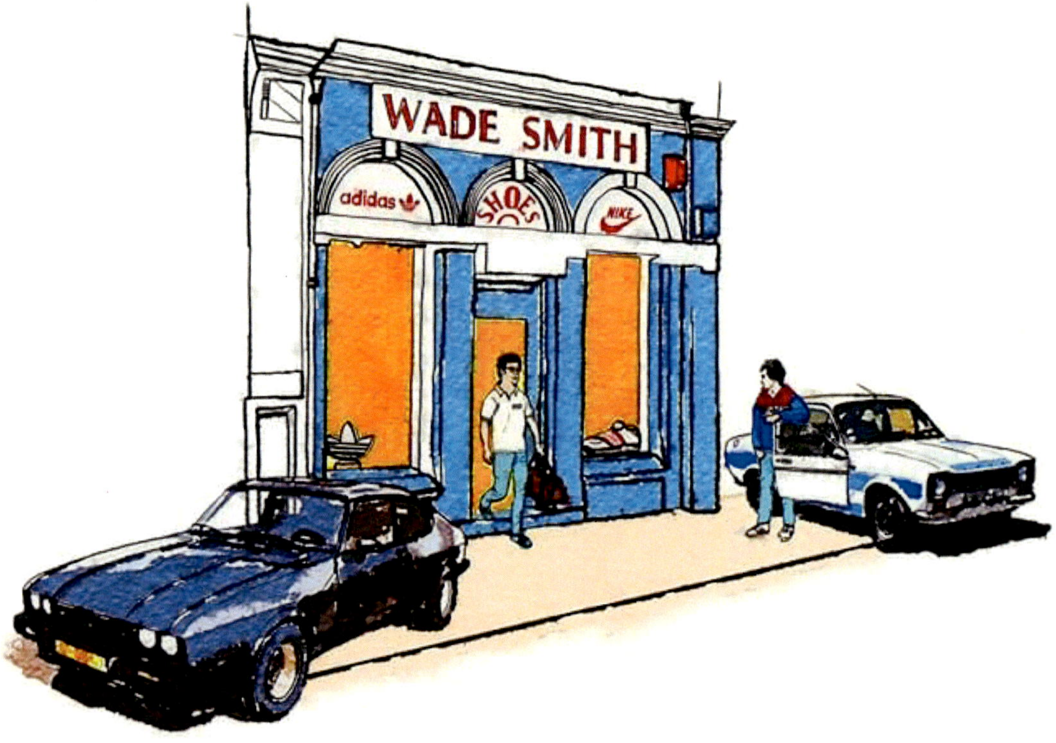

The adidas Trimm-Trab ended up accounting for 80% of Wade Smith's total sales in its first year. Getting the store up and running had been an ambition of Robert's since the age of 15. He had been controller of the 20 adidas concessions by the late 1970s. For 18 months, arguments with adidas big wigs over the supply of new styles to Liverpool ended with Robert being pushed out of his controllers' job at the adidas concession stores. He knew the kids on Merseyside were willing to pay big bucks for the latest adidas but it was just 'a passing phase' according to some. adidas had over 200 designs globally but only supplied the U.K. with some 40. They assumed the newer more expensive trainers were too expensive for the U.K. market. Robert knew otherwise.

The Wade Smith store was now on the map. In Aachen, West Germany, there was a main adidas retailer and Robert withdraws the total amount of his overdraft, hires a van and travels over. He is able to buy 475 pairs of trainers. Before long, the shop is importing shoes from Germany, France, Austria and Ireland. Within seven weeks, the store had sold £27000 worth of trainers. The years of 1981 and 1982 were to be the pinnacle of the cult for rare trainers. Even during the early days of Wade Smith, Robert would actually fall out of favour with adidas and its UK distributors. He was parallel importing the brand because the UK distributor could not supply the much needed expensive shoes and with being from the UK he was not allowed to buy direct from adidas Germany, France or Belgium. Robert 'If I was buying 400 pair at a time from European retailers, I would get 20% discount. In fact one retailer from Munich would just add 10% to his cost. So I was getting nearer and nearer to the cost from adidas Germany. And the cost in Germany was actually a lot less than the cost in the UK. So I had to break a few of the distribution rules and fall out with some people but you generally do when you are building a business.'

It soon became apparent to the seasoned travellers that Robert was able to get his own trainers. Now they started offering him the top makes of sportswear, t-shirts, sweatshirts and tracksuits.

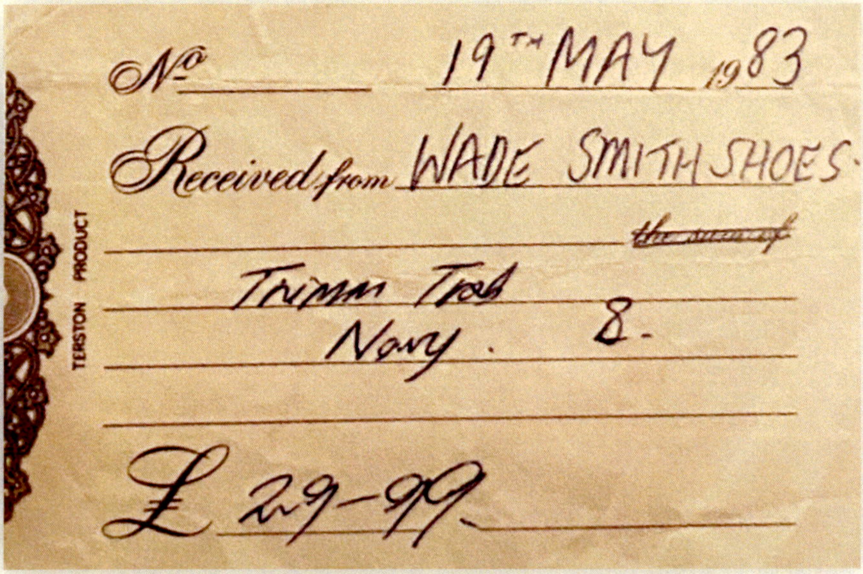
No 19TH MAY 1983

Received from WADE SMITH SHOES.

~~the sum of~~

Trimm Trab

Navy. 8.

£ 29-99.

TERSTON PRODUCT

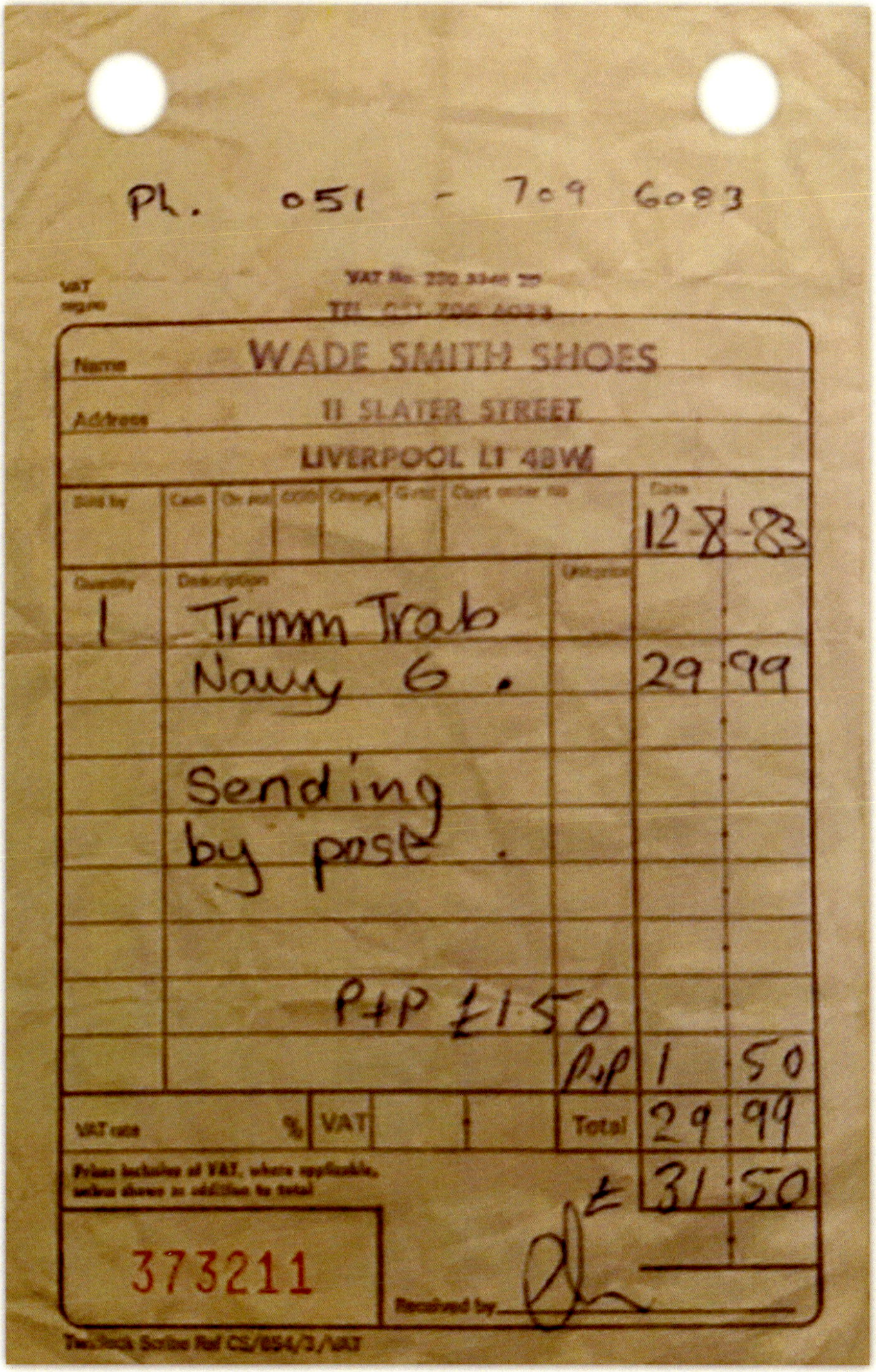

Ph. 051 - 709 6083

VAT regno

VAT No. 232 3340 37
TEL. 051 709 6083

Name	WADE SMITH SHOES
Address	11 SLATER STREET
	LIVERPOOL L1 4BW

Sold by	Cash	On acc	C.O.D.	Charge	Cust order no	Date
						12-8-83

Quantity	Description	Unit price	£
1	Trimm Trab		
	Navy 6.		29 99
	Sending by post.		
	P+P £1.50		
		P+P	1 50
VAT rate %	VAT	Total	29 99
Prices inclusive of VAT, where applicable, unless shown as addition to total		£	31 50

373211

Received by

Twinlock Scribe Ref CS/654/3/VAT

Robert, 'I certainly think that with the Liverpool fans travelling around Europe it opened up the whole phase for getting rare trainers because it was brilliant the fact that you couldn't get them in the UK. That's what made them more desirable. So there was a race all the time. Some people might go to London to get a pair of Diadora Bjorn Borgs Elite Trainers, because professionals like Borg and John McEnroe did set a trend for expensive tennis trainers, expensive tops, tracksuits, or whatever McEnroe was wearing. But obviously non of that expensive Italian sportswear was available in the U.K. so there was a race to, not just go to Lilywhites in London but the Liverpudlians were travelling around Europe and so would go to the big sports shops in Munich, Milan etc to bring back as much expensive gear as possible. They'd sell it to their mates which paid for their next trip. So there was a lot of trading going on amongst the Liverpudlians with the gear that they brought back that would help to pay for the next trip. I mean how many trips did Liverpool make in that five year period from 1977-82?'

With expectations of selling maybe £26,000 worth of shoes in the first year, the shop ended up selling £110,000 worth. Of the years Wade Smith was operated on Slater Street the trainer cult was to peak in 1984.

Robert 'Our peak trainer year was 1984-85. I think we did over £500,000 worth of sales in a back street shop in Liverpool. I seem to remember paying my whole years rent on Easter Saturday in 1984, which was an incredible thing. If you can imagine £10,000 a week selling trainers out of a back street shop in 1984, it was a remarkable time. I mean I had been earning about £4000 to £5000 a year as a rep for adidas but I think within three years by the time I was 23/24 we were making more than £100,000 net out of Slater Street. So that was the vintage year 84/85. It was the last vintage year, if you like, for the cult and after that it became mainstream and it spread across the UK and the rest of the World really and Nike and Reebok helped to stretch it into mainstream business really.'

It wouldn't be long before a bigger store is needed to stock the goods for his expanding empire. That store ended up being on Lord Street before eventually he takes over the Glacier/Chicago Buildings close to Mathew Street. Chris Lee worked in Wade Smith and recalls how exciting it was to just see the latest adidas catalogue. 'It was a great place to work, especially when getting the latest catalogues from Germany but also opening boxes from the delivery of hundreds of pristine pairs of trainers. Sometimes stuff would arrive from a German retailer. The guy would try and save some money by switching a pair we'd ordered to another pair he couldn't sell, but the best part for us was finding he'd put in a rare pair of adidas we could sell for a better price'

To give some sort of indication of how big the Wade Smith trainer phenomena grew, Robert explains how the Marathon TR sold in exceptional numbers. 'As the years went by, in the 80s, the fashion moved across into top running shoes and we had a massive year in 1984-85 with a shoe called the Marathon TR which had the adidas logo on the sole. It had been around since the late 70s as the best running shoe in the World, supposedly, but didn't sell. A few years later I found 3000 pairs in Ireland of all places. I bought every pair for almost a tenner each. I shouldn't say this but we basically nicked them off the Irish distributor. He had been sitting on them for three years in his warehouse in Cork. Michael O'Connor was a lovely guy, and I think I bought five hundred pairs and went back for the rest. £15 a pair to start with, then I bought two thousand pairs at £10. That was the last big cult adidas trainer of the 80s. I then sold, would you believe, the 3000 pairs at £35 a pair in one shop. That must be a record in the world for any one shop to sell such an amount. I mean who sells 3000 pairs of one style?'

As the insurmountable demand for trainers catapulted Wade Smith's profile, the cost soon began to increase. The pigskin Zelda was the first $100 trainer in the World. Robert tells us 'Reebok think they invented the garment leather. The glove leather shoe with their leather Reebok Classics and the Workouts but adidas had already invented it a few years earlier.

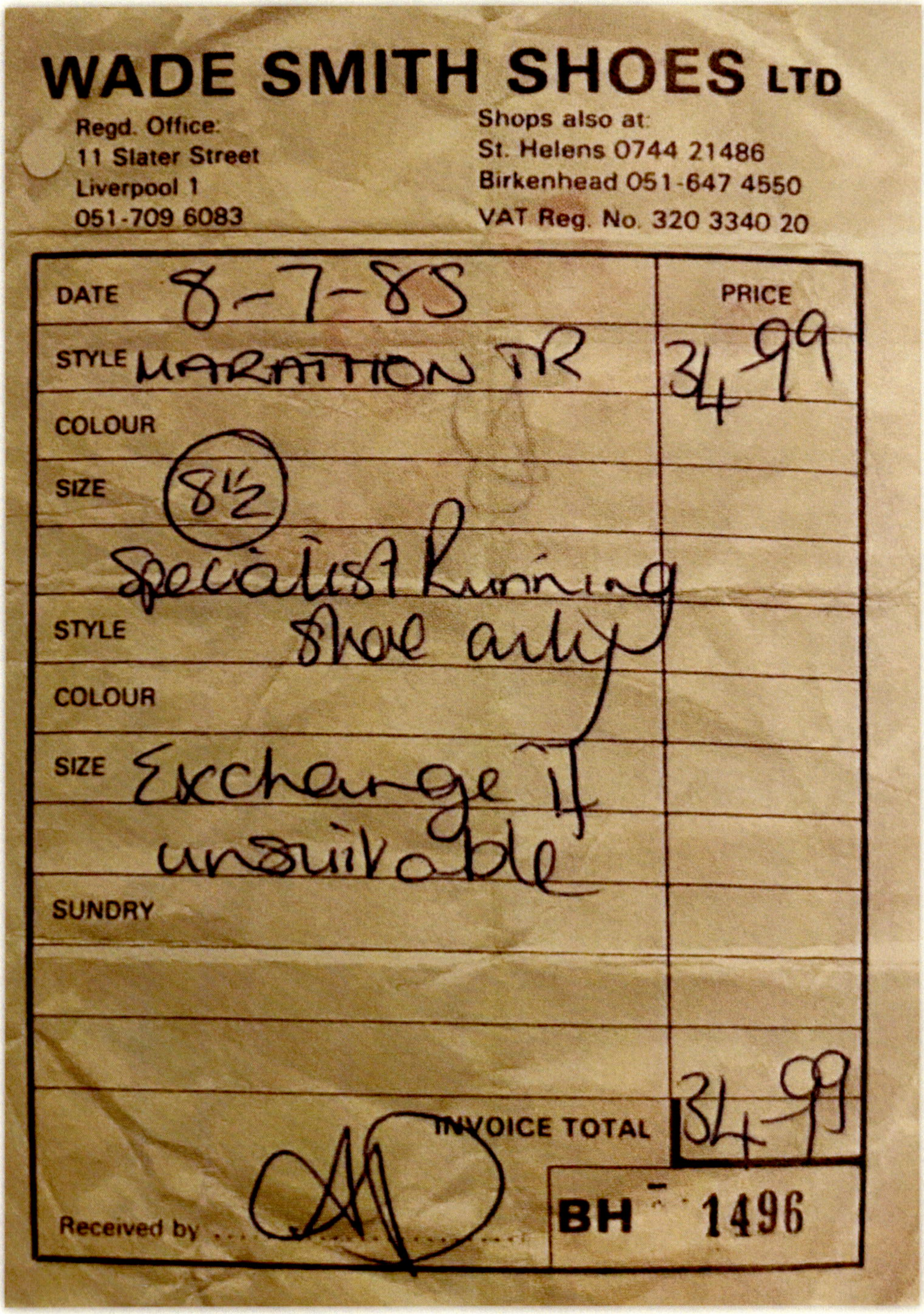
WADE SMITH SHOES LTD

Regd. Office:
11 Slater Street
Liverpool 1
051-709 6083

Shops also at:
St. Helens 0744 21486
Birkenhead 051-647 4550
VAT Reg. No. 320 3340 20

	PRICE
DATE 8-7-85	
STYLE MARATHON TR	34.99
COLOUR	
SIZE 8½	
specialist running	
STYLE shoe only	
COLOUR	
SIZE Exchange if	
unsuitable	
SUNDRY	
INVOICE TOTAL	34.99

Received by ....

BH - 1496

They didn't sell very well, especially in America, but we ended up selling the last of the 1982 stock at Wade Smith. This was a £50 shoe in 1982. So Liverpool took it to new levels. It began to spread when I started Wade Smith. I went from 50 styles to over 150 styles of adidas shoes from all over the world in that first year. And that was my big break from taking it from a wall of trainers, to four walls of trainers in a shop with the biggest range of fashion trainers pretty much on the planet at that time. I knew where to get the stock from in Germany and France, plus imports from Ireland and we were even bringing stuff over from the States. Anything we could get our hands on in terms of imports. adidas had factories in France, Germany, Austria and Yugoslavia, so production was coming from all over the place. They tended to have a separate range for France, a separate range for Germany and I suppose I brought all those different ranges into the shop for the first time.'

The uniqueness of having different models of adidas had waned by the late 80s. The trainers had been made in such countries as France, West Germany, Austria or Yugoslavia and each had their own styles suitable to their own sales market, but in the mid 80s adidas had moved production to China and the Far East with each model being produced for a World market at a considerably cheaper price than in Europe.

Even so, by the end of the 80s Wade Smith had become firmly entrenched in Liverpool fashion. Robert's ultimate aspiration was to own a building similar to Barneys Luxury Department Store in New York. The first step would be the opening of the Mathew Street branch which had 4 floors with a basement for storage. It was here that worldwide luxury brands would be introduced to everyone from young kids to millionaire footballers. Robert again 'At our peak we had fifty brands from all around the world, all the best brands. But eighty per cent of the business was coming from the top twelve mega brands. I was always a bit uncomfortable with it but that was the reality and like I say as soon as the brands wanted their own stores that really was the end of Wade Smith.'

At first business boomed in its new Store. Robert 'We opened a floor a year in that building right through the 90s and can you believe turn over was a million pounds in 1989. By 1995 I think we made around seven or eight million pounds in that five year period in sales in one building consisting of five floors. We then opened the sportswear building and the junior building and it all started to grow too quickly.' But the Arcadia Group still made an offer for the company in 1998. A fee of £17.3million changed hands and the owners of TopShop and Burton became the new proprietors.

Robert on the 90s designer boom. 'I don't think anybody could imagine how big the whole cult of the 80s and 90s designer label thing would become. In fact it became too big really. The bubble did burst in the late 90s. Maybe it was the silly prices for top end labels, which created an anti-brand thing.'

A lot of people headed back to the High Street. For the women there was the re-emergence of Top Shop and Primark appeared on the scene with its throw-away fashion. Designs seen on the catwalks of Milan and Paris could be copied and in their Stores within two months. Top models and footballers wives would be seen with a Top Shop or Primark bag, giving the stores much needed credibility.

Robert bought back the business from Arcadia for £7m in 2001. But its glory days had passed. Robert 'I felt it was important to get the Wade Smith brand back and maybe downsize the Store to a smaller space, like the original Matthew Street store, before its expansion across the building.'

The dynamic had changed though over those last few years. Brands began opening their own Stores in Cities up and down the Country. The exclusivity of only being able to pick up a certain label from Wade Smith had disappeared. Wade Smith closed its doors in 2005 as the bank was unwilling to provide any more financial backing. The High Street was also struggling with the emergence of the internet and online buying.

Bespoke Tailoring

Bespoke is custom made to order. Liverpool has always had its fair share of tailors, many surviving since the drape suits of the 1950s. Today Bespoke Tailoring accounts for quality and style. Saville Row in London has had an influx of young designers already at the top of their profession opening bespoke shops to supply those who want the best. This discerning customer wants that bit of individuality that comes with a custom made suit, jacket or even shoes. In 1981, that individuality was present in many, and soon a young crowd of individuals requiring at first leather jackets would frequent some of Liverpools Master Tailors. Rob and Chris Davies on Whitechapel became the obligatory tailor to this young crowd. Word spread but only those with a bit of cash could afford to have a jacket made. A hand made jacket wasn't something you could rob from a shop and long gone were the days when spivs sold cloth by the yard in the local pub.

Tony had a job and so could afford something costing a few bob. 'The first jacket I had made was a blouson by Rob Davies, who at the time was on Cases Street, it cost me about £90 but soon the style had changed and a Hunter style jacket was 'IN', thigh length with an elasticated waist, it cost about £140. I also had a cord jacket made. Lori Larty from Lori and the Chameleons had a small shop next to Zoo Records and I had to buy the cord material and she put it together.' Within a year, a bespoke suit for that special occasion was also needed. Many mates were turning 18 and it soon became fashionable to have a suit or just a pair of trousers made to order. I had a suit and two pairs of trousers made by Monty Fagin on Dale Street. The mate Steven would go to Peter Harland on Victoria Street and once put a £40 deposit down on a £200 suit, but then realised he couldn't really afford it and so lost his deposit. The pants would be worn a lot, especially at weekends, but I think the jacket only came out for special occasions.

This was obviously well before all of the designer stores offered ready to wear suits of the quality and style wanted at the time. Horne Bros and Watson Prickard were just two of the places to offer ready made suits, but it was only when places such as Wade Smith had expanded to offer Italian and continental style suits that the suit would return to favour. The originality of the bespoke suit more or less died as more stores like Harold Ian and Giorgio began offering styles from abroad. Giorgio on Mount Pleasant were the first store to offer Giorgio Armani in the U.K. Their range of suits and shirts were the only attire for sale as the more casual Armani Jeans line was still a few years away.

The Pubs & Clubs

Although the Roxy/Bowie style had transferred the Wedge hairstyle from a couple of night clubs to the terraces, music failed to have any more influence on the clothes and styles being worn on matchday. A few Punks and Mods attended games but eventually they would have their hair re-shaped Wedge style. In the centre of Liverpool, certain pubs and clubs became the 'IN' place to be seen. Punk music was new and original and took the helm from Roxy and Bowie. Erics for the matinee shows [under 16's] on a Saturday afternoon became a riot of pogo-ing kids. Most acts booked for the Saturday night usually performed a matinee show in the afternoon. The entrance fee was never more than a pound and the matinee usually started at 5.00pm. Sometimes the kids would be getting chased out while the queue was forming outside for the night show. Many acts that went on to bigger things started out at places like Erics on Mathew Street. The Clash, The Skids, Magazine, The Undertones and Elvis Costello all did matinee shows. The Clash gig in July 1978 supported by The Specials was a bonus after the Empire got cold feet due to the irresponsible behaviour of many punks at gigs nationwide.

Erics had opened in October 1976 and straight away became the focal point for most up and coming bands. Now remembered as one of the greatest Punk clubs of all time, many elitist Punks will need reminding that there was another crowd that turned up every week. 'Scottie one eyes' was the name given by the punks to the match going lads who went to the club to listen to the live acts on the underground stage. The 'Scottie' coming from Scotland Road and 'one eyes' taken from the wedge hairstyle covering one eye. There never seemed to be much conflict, due to the mutual admiration for the music.

The matinees would sometimes start early afternoon, if the groups arrived Midday, therefore it was possible to take in an early show before jumping the bus up to Anfield or Goodison for the afternoon game. Yes, these were the days of 3 o'clock Kick Offs on a Saturday. The only occasion the time was changed was if the game coincided with the Grand National. Then it was usually an 11.00 K.O.

By 1978 the youngsters at the forefront of this new culture were looking at the City nightlife now instead of the under 16 or 18 discos. On leaving school at 16, there was always one or two clubs in the City Centre that would be welcoming. Erics was always worth a visit when a decent group was on. The Swinging Apple on Wood Street was a Punk haunt that attracted many who enjoyed the music and Checkmate down the road was playing the Bowie/Roxy sounds. Two dance floors were intended to keep the 'straights' and 'Bowie pants' apart but the air was often filled with the threat of violence. The Apple sometimes attracted an unruly element and often gangs of Scally's went to the Club looking for trouble with the anarchic tribe. Punks were getting used to thisanimosity. Probe on Button Street every Saturday became an epicentre for a variety of cultures. Punks, Teds/Rockabillies and even Mods ventured to the area around Probe to hang out. Fights often breaking out between the different factions. Probe was a fantastic Independent Record Shop and the only place to get any new releases, whether it was on 7", 12", picture disc, gatefold sleeve, flexi-disc or a 10" flexi picture disc in a gatefold sleeve. Probe usually had it first. The buying of records also had its one-upmanship with the purchase needing to be done on the day of release and the Limited Edition recording being the first choice. Being served by the outrageous Pete Burns of Dead or Alive with his black contact lenses in, could give anyone nightmares though.

Although there was no link between the music and the terraces, many faces from the games began doing the same round of Pubs and Clubs. The Apple was an end of night favourite for its mix of Punk, New Wave and even Reggae music, which kept the Skinheads happy.

If there was a game in London on the Saturday and the Bright and Early was booked, then an all night drink was to be had in The Timepiece downstairs, once the Apple had shut at 2.00a.m. If not there, then it was down to the Night Owl just off Stanley Street. If there was no game, it was the Pier Head for a bacon buttie and the first bus home at around 6.30a.m. 1979/80 saw Mod and Ska music being embraced with groups such as The Jam, The Specials and Madness. These groups hit the big time quite quickly and so the only places to see them would be, the Empire, Royal Court or Mountford Hall. Especially after Erics closed its doors on 14th March 1980 due to consistent police pressure.

Also, the early sounds of electronic music with Kraftwerk, the Human League and Cabaret Voltaire began filtering into D.J. sets in places like the Harrington. A lot of Pubs and Clubs became popular due to this music. Yet again, many of those faces who went the game were the main clientele. The same faces were seen in the same half dozen pubs between Dale Street and Harrington Street.

A regular pub-crawl for us would start by jumping off the bus by The Cunarder or The Shakespeare on Roe Street. In the Cunarder, we would listen to a couple of songs [The Undertones, The Boomtown Rats,] from the Irish Top Ten on the jukebox and then head off towards Daleys on Dale Street. A game of Spacies [Space Invaders] or maybe a game of Pool. I remember Daleys Dandelion had the glass table top Space Invaders as well as the usually upright machine. After a few games and listening to Suzanne by Leonard Cohen on the jukebox half a dozen times, it was time to move on to Rigbys opposite, then up the side street [Hackins Hey] to Scarletts Bar. From there, it was across to Cook Street and The Vaults. The Pubs on Harrington Street were also regular haunts. The Why Not, The Crocodile and The Pen and Wig were only up the road from the Harrington Bar. The night was seen out at the Harrington. The Pen and Wig had a pool table and was even advertised in the Liverpool Echo for having pool and darts. The jukebox in the Why Not carried a few classics.

The Pubs with the best jukeboxes were always a good draw on a weekend Pub crawl. At the Harrington, the D.J. played all the latest music whether it was the Clash [White Man In Hammersmith Palais] or early The Human League [Being Boiled] mixed with classics including Bowie [Kooks, Queen Bitch] or Iggy Pop [Passenger]. The crowd was a mix. It had been a gay bar in the early days and still had one or two of that persuasion. Probably the first place you would see eye make-up on a lad. Now if you thought Pete Burns was scary, this was even more so. Plus, there were a couple of Mods and many Bowie disciples. These usually stayed close to the dance floor preening themselves in the mirror. Downstairs was a haven of smartly dressed football followers, but considering this mixed bunch there was hardly any trouble. The thought of trouble must have been on the managements mind though due to the ale being served in plastic glasses. If a night of bother was what you were after, there was no better place than Gatsbys on Victoria Street. With its disco dance floor and Genesis corner, it was always a bit of an edgy place. Usually more fighting than dancing.

Across town on Hardman Street was for the posers. Places to catch a glimpse of these beauts were Chaucers, Plummers and Kirklands. There always seemed to be an over-21 door policy at these places or you needed a tie and jacket. Maybe it was to stop any football riff-raff from getting in. Certainly seemed to work, so most lads kept to the other side of town.

Home match days saw many mobs converge into the Pubs around Lime Street in anticipation of away supporters leaving the Station. The Sportsman [later to be called Quinns] with its racing car hanging from the ceiling was next to the Royal Court and The Star and Garter opposite Lime Street were quickly accessible to the Station via the subway under the road. The Yankee Bar on Lime Street itself was a big favourite before and after home or away games. The bar had a pole rising up from the floor and it wasn't uncommon for drunken regulars to attempt a quick scaling to punch the ceiling. To put a stop to this the owners eventually greased the top of the pole. Similar drunken attempts to get into the Sports Car in The Sportsman would have the audience in stitches.

'GOT THE TIME ON YER?' and 3/4 TIME

The whole culture centred around the match. The latest styles could be checked out and the ground became a meeting place. To be involved in the whole scene meant going to the game. A bit like the Mods going to the seaside every Bank Holiday. Only this wasn't every now and then, it was every week. It would be impossible to mention the Casual culture and clothes without bringing the match into the equation. Then the hooliganism needs a small mention, as would the Mod riots if talking about Mod culture.

Hooliganism reared its ugly head during the early 1970's. Grounds weren't segregated and so there was a home end and the opposite end was for any away fans that cared to attend. Problem therefore was home fans congregating in this end as well. Home hooligans would go into the part of the ground were the away fans had gathered. Their territory was being invaded. Trouble would arise until the police moved in. On other occasions, pitch invasions by one set of fans trying to get at the opposition fans caused games to be held up. It was obvious something had to be done to curb such antics.

By 1975, Manchester United had gained a reputation, as an unruly crowd, intent on causing problems wherever they played. Liverpool's game in November of this year gave cause for concern. It was decided to keep the Manchester fans segregated from the Liverpool supporters in the Anfield Road End. Two five feet high walls of tubular steel was erected down the centre of the terraces with a three foot gap in between for Inspector Blackbeard and his officers to patrol. The wall became a permanent fixture, but was only used for the penning-in of United supporters. That was until a few years later when the Road End was divided again into two quarters. All away fans now had their own section.

In 1977, fencing around the whole perimeter of the pitch was erected to stop any pitch invasions. The hooliganism inside of the grounds had now been sorted. What happened now was the trouble moved outside into the surrounding streets close to the stadiums. The hooligans now prepared themselves for battling outside the grounds.

During the 1960s, before travelling to away games became popular, some Liverpool and Everton fans alternated between going to Anfield and Goodison. In the period of Samba and Stan Smith, something similar arose. Three Quarter time, as it became known, was the period when the gates at the grounds were opened to let those out, who wanted to beat the rush home. With 10-15 minutes of the game left, the Road End/Park End would suddenly seem twice as full. What was happening was, Blues would come up to Anfield to team up with their mates for any after match shenanigans and vice versa. The mob that the away fans had been a bit wary of, had apparently grown larger. The short trip to the coach or car on Priory or Pinehurst or the even longer journey to Lime Street was now looking very dodgy. As the away fans were kept in, hundreds of yobs would gather by the Arkles and in Stanley Park in readiness to pick off their prey. It was the obligatory thing to do and was a ritual that lasted years for many. Once the away fans were let out, things got decidedly naughty. Any going to their cars were soon picked out, either by the clothes being worn or the accent on replying to being asked the time.

Once or twice Liverpool woolly backs took a beating for speaking with the wrong accent. There was a certain whistle that could be heard from the Scallys who were on to someone and soon a larger mob was after them. As soon as a skirmish occurred, the sound of police sirens and the screech of black mariahs would send the mob scurrying in all directions. Eric 'On one occasion, two Leeds fans were walking down Utting Avenue. They were quickly sussed and the obvious question was aired 'Got the time on yer?' 'Errm, twenty past nine, wack' was the comical reply.

'Where are yer from?' someone else enquires. One of the Leeds lads quickly looks up at an approaching 17c bus and replies 'Errm Faz...zack...erk...ley.' I think they realised what was about to happen, so as everyone was rolling on the floor laughing, they sped off down a side street. When we caught up with them, they were trying to get into a cab, but the cab driver was having none of it. As a few of the lads threw a few digs in, the cab driver could be heard shouting 'Watch the taxi lads' The beating wasn't too severe, they weren't proper Leeds hooligans and they just happened to be in the wrong place at the wrong time. It was something that could happen to anyone who didn't have their wits about them when going to an away game. They were also relieved of their watches.' This ritual dates back to the skinheads from the early 70s who would follow any away supporters who turned up at Lime Street and relinquish them of their sheepskin coats, jewellery and even shoes on some occasions.

Away Travel

There was only two main options really when travelling to an away game. The 'Special' and the 'Ordinary' were both associated with the lifestyle of the new culture. The Football Special was the organised train. A joint promotion by the Football Clubs and British Rail. It was usually manned by police or Club stewards and would be met by a police escort to the ground. Then you had the Inter City trains, which were known as the Ordinary. These were the daily excursions to and from Cities all over Britain. They would become the popular choice of most Clubs fans. The Ordinary trains gave more freedom of choice when arriving at its destination and didn't usually have any police travelling on them.

Coaches were used in limited quantities, especially by Liverpool and Everton fans, at the time. If you knew you were going to be met at an away ground by hundreds baying for your blood, it was best to arrive in numbers and not on a 50 seated bus. By 1978, a new breed of hooligan had taken over. They were now, a younger, more stylised group that attracted huge numbers. The glamour of the well-turned out mob saw numbers multiply and soon the only option for everyone was to stay together and travel mob handed. Travelling by car was definitely off the agenda.. Straight jeans and trainees had been given the seal of approval.

The Special

The Football Special was British Rails idea of transportation. A means to an end really. It usually got you to your match destination in time for kick-off but no guarantees were given on arriving back in Lime Street on time. British Rail rolled out it's dated engines to pull supporters up and down the country every match day.

FOOTBALL TRIPS

SATURDAY 15 MARCH, 1980 BRISTOL CITY V
LIVERPOOL AT ASHTON GATE K.O. 15.00

In connection with the above, a Special Train has been arranged as under:-

OUTWARDS	PINK TICKETS	RETURN FARE
Liverpool Lime St.	dep 10.15	£6.00
Parson St. (Bristol)	arr 14.10	

RETURN		
Parson St. (Bristol)	dep 17.20	
Liverpool Lime St.	arr 21.29	

On the return journey, the train will call at Runcorn, Allerton, Mossley Hill and Edge Hill for the convenience of passengers wishing to alight at these stations.

If this train does not run, owing to the match being cancelled or postponed, your rail ticket will become invalid and must be returned within 14 days for a full refund. It will not be valid for the re-arranged date.

Further information will be supplied on application to Stations or Telephone 709-9696.

Travelling to away games really came to the fore during the 1960s. Work was aplenty and the economy was good. Many youths held down a job and with money in their pockets they were able to afford to go to the game with their mates. Tickets to the matches were also affordable and easy to acquire, and before long Britain began to witness travelling supporters. British Rail soon noticed the money making potential of putting on extra trains to transport the fans. One problem that was soon to arise was the ideas of challenge and territory. The 60s saw this breed of travelling supporter coincide with the rise of the skinhead movement. Renowned for causing trouble, more and more grounds began seeing organised gangs at the games with the intention of causing as much agro as possible. The Football Special was born but the problem was, many of these trouble causers were in the same spot at the same time. Usually on these trains. The old engines on the trains meant slow, long, tedious journeys and the boring trips soon riled many. The history of wrecked carriages, usually highlighted on TV Programmes like Look North or Nationwide in the evenings, soon put paid to fans travelling unsupervised. The fact that Everton fans were able to pull off a carriage door was soon transformed into a standing joke whenever a comedian appeared on Merseyside. In September 1975, British Rail pulled the plug on the Football Special for the remainder of that season amid the growing problems of football hooliganism. By the end of the 1970s police or Club stewards would be manned on each train. It wouldn't be long before 'herded' and 'cattle' were being heard in the same sentence. The worst crime ended up being a few light bulbs and beer cans being launched out of the windows on passing through a Station. Trainspotters, usually at Crewe, became the obvious target.

Tickets for the train went on sale the week of the game. British Rail had the right to put on any number of trains. If one train sold out another could be added depending on demand. It was advisable to get a ticket early to avoid the disappointment of the train selling out and them not putting on another.

The talk all week would be how many were going to the away game. How many Specials were going and how many were on the Ordinary. In the early days of the Special it was possible to take cans of ale onto the trains but at the start of the 1980/81 season British Rail introduced the 'dry' Special. The train schedule had the warning 'You must note specially that the taking of intoxicating liquor onto all vehicles of this train is prohibited.' Hooliganism was at its peak and the powers that be were trying every avenue to curb the troublemakers. On arriving at its final destination the train would be met by a police escort with dogs and black mariahs to stop fans going to Pubs or rampaging through the streets. The return train home always seemed fuller than going out. This was mainly due to those on the Ordinary wanting to get home earlier rather than having to wait around for their own train.

The 1981/82 Season saw the introduction of a reduced fare for Young Person Railcard Holders.

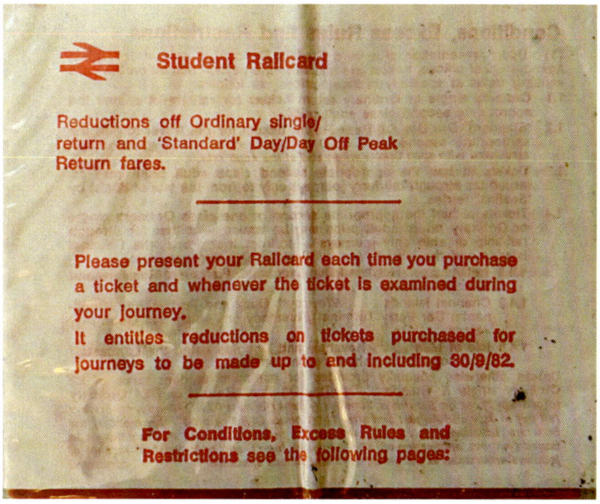
Student Railcard

Reductions off Ordinary single/ return and 'Standard' Day/Day Off Peak Return fares.

Please present your Railcard each time you purchase a ticket and whenever the ticket is examined during your journey.
It entitles reductions on tickets purchased for journeys to be made up to and including 30/9/82.

For Conditions, Excess Rules and Restrictions see the following pages:

Although there hadn't been any reductions before for children or O.A.Ps this was an ideal opportunity for some to save a few bob. My mate was at college and he had one of these railcards. I purchased it from him and replaced his picture with mine. I saved a bit of money that season. The reduction was usually around 25%, £1.50 or £2 depending on the journey. Sunderland £4.50 instead of £6, Chelsea and West Ham £6 instead of £8.

The train consisted of two types of carriage, first and second class. The first class compartment had six seats and the added luxury of a wire luggage rack, ideal for getting your head down on lengthy journeys. Most notably the 1977 European Cup Final [2 days there, 3 days back] and then from places such as Southend and Aberdeen. Not the most comfortable of beds though. The seats were usually filled with the wools [woolly-backs] that had been queuing up for hours to get on the train first at platform 9. The second-class seats filled a whole carriage. Most had a table between the seats, ideal for the card school. Whole carriages could be taken up by firms from different areas of Liverpool, Huyton, Breck Road, Halewood etc. An hour into the journey and a toss of a coin would decide who was going to queue for an hour at the buffet car. An appetising selection of Robirch pies or a Mars/Marathon bar was on the menu. Although the Aberdeen game, besides being famous as the game that introduced the Casuals styles to Scotland, was also best remembered for the egg and chips on offer on the train. Either that or bring your own butties wrapped in a Mothers Pride bread bag. Alan 'I remember the 'Special' breaking down on the way to Derby. I leant out of the window for a bit of fresh air and all I could see strewn across the track for a hundred yards were loads of empty Mothers Pride wrappers.'

Under seat heating was on hand, it usually worked on hot days and was broke on cold days. The cold days usually being a midweek winter fixture were you arrived home after midnight. A long haul trip to Ipswich springs to mind and these were the days of only wearing a t-shirt or shirt and no coat. On arrival at the destination, a police escort would meet the train. Fans would have to queue before being frog-marched to the ground. Although the 'Special' could be full of wools, many 'Boys' still used the train. These would be the ones looking to 'break out' of the escort if any confrontation was to arise. Also, should a mob be waiting, it became the norm for the well dressed to be to the outside of the escort. This was to show the opposing supporters how much better dressed we were. Cries of the classic 'There's a woolly over there, and he's wearing brown airwear,' rang out at most grounds.

Travelling by 'Special' was a safe option in these times. There would be a group of 3/400 on each train and such a large amount being escorted by police led to a bit of complacency. Being better dressed and in large numbers made many feel un-touchable and at most grounds Scousers were. One occasion though which has gone down in folklore was the visit to Tottenham in the Quarter Final of the F.A.Cup in March 1980. The game was on a Saturday with Tottenham being the only London club playing at home that day. It looked a potential hazard straight away. Cockneys hate Scousers and vice versa. The train schedule stated passengers would have to make their own way from Euston to Seven Sisters via the Underground. No problem there, 300 on the 'special' staying together should be a big enough defence.

The journey to the ground passed off without much incident. A few shouts and songs directed at any Spurs standing in pub doorways. Plenty of MA1's on show, a firm favourite with London Skinheads and lots of Donkey Jackets. The Donkey Jacket being a relic from the traditional Skins of the early 70's. After the game was another story.

Terry McDermott scored the 'Goal of the Season' to give the Reds a 1-0 win. On leaving the ground, the police had made a cordon across the end of the road. This was to be the front of the escort back to Seven Sisters Tube Station. Opposite was every hooligan from every Club in London. As the escort started it's treacherous journey along the road, it soon became clear that the police were only protecting those at the front. Skins, Punks and all were making their way into the escort, Scuffles would break out at the back, and the police would run from the front to the back. Those at the front were then attacked, the police were back and forth for what seemed an eternity. 10000 Liverpool started in the escort, by the time we reached the Station, about 200 were left. I remember thinking 'Thank god we've made it' and then on going down into the tube there were Tottenham down there. Enough was enough, these foolish few were chased by the 200 that had stayed together. The mate had his Campri coat wrecked, others licked their wounds, but we all lived to tell the tale for years to come. There would be no hiding place that day for the design obsessed. Not even the best of Cockney accents would have helped if you were dressed in the latest baggy jeans with Stan Smith or Kickers on your feet.

THE ORDINARY 'Bright and Early' and Persil

The Inter City trains became the preferred method of transport for away games by the late 70s. Policing fans arriving in Town was increasingly difficult. The 'Ordinary', as it became known, gave the new mobs the freedom to arrive where and when they wanted. One popular train was the 'Bright and Early'. The 06.22am to London Euston on a Saturday arrived in the Capital at around 09.30am. Many jumping this early train would be the worse for wear after all night drinking sessions in some after hours club. There was then plenty of time to pay a visit to such places as Lillywhites, Dickie Dirts, Benneton, Harrods or the Lonsdale Boxing shop.

With Liverpool in the capital so many times in this period, a couple of pubs close to Euston became regular meeting places before and after games. The Somers and the Lion and Lamb heaved every weekend when the Scousers were in town. A tap on the window and the doors were opened up early. After the games and it was back to the pub until the last train back home. Another option was the 'Post train'. Leaving at Midnight on the Friday, the journey was an enduring 6 hours, giving plenty of time for a short nap. Once hitting the capital the Fruit Market Bar was always open for first orders with drinks available till around 8.30a.m for its early morning workers. In 1980, fans on Merseyside became the cleanest as well as the best dressed in the league. Persil came up with a fine marketing ploy. If enough tokens were collected from the tops of Persil boxes, they could be exchanged for 'Two for One Rail Tickets'. This now enticed more people to travel on 'The Ordinary'. Chris travelled to London regularly on shopping sprees, but only after his ma had used enough Persil for him to get Two for One Tickets.

British Rail (M)
Return
Manchester Saver
2nd Period Return
To Manchester (Victoria)
From Liverpool (Lime St.)
via Earlestown
Issued subject to the Regulations and Conditions in the Publications and Notices of the British Railways Board.
Not Transferable.
BR4563/216
Valid by Authorised trains
(See over)
(No 1)
Date of Outward travel
10 APR 82
Valid for Return travel any day within one calendar month of date shown.
Adult
№ 8641
Outward

The Retro-Scal

The start of the 1981/82 Season saw changes both on and off the pitch. Jimmy Hill came up with the idea of three points for a win, which was duly introduced. Also, Terry Venables introduced a synthetic surface to Loftus Road, which eventually helped Q.P.R. reach the F.A. Cup Final. Things were also changing on the fashion stakes.

As 1982 approached, the dress code on Merseyside went off in two directions. Whether this had anything to do with Liverpools early exit from Europe is anyones guess, or could it be that familiarity bred contempt as every man and his dog was onto the Casual look. A new 'Retro-Scal' or 'Scruff' look took a hold, centred around cannabis and a love of pre-eighties progressive dinosaur music. It seemed that if you listened to Pink Floyd, Gabriel's Genesis, Zappa or Liverpool's very own Groundpig with their covers of the above plus a surreal rendition of Postman Pat, then you needed a joint between your fingers. The clothes almost became a second thought. Enter a Sold Out Groundpig gig at any pub, Hofbrauhaus on Mount Pleasant was a regular joint, and it was as though a Geography teachers Convention was taking place. The clothes although new were decidedly downbeat. Tweed and Corduroy Jackets complimented with Hush Puppies and faded Levi's. Genesis and Floyd T-Shirts were a must. Gatsby's on Victoria Street even had its own 'Genesis Corner' where it was possible to light up until the manageress politely told everyone to 'put the spliffs out'. It was even possible to have smoke in a quiet corner downstairs in the Harrington Bar.

Pot film classics such as 'Up In Smoke' starring Cheech and Chong plus Floyds 'The Wall' were being constantly played on the new £300 VHS and Betamax video systems that had revolutionised the watching of T.V. Many second hand record stores reported un-precedented sales of L.P.'s by said artists as the Culture spread throughout Merseyside. This was a new post Casual culture all of its own. An underground cult, yet to be fully documented.

Peter Hooton has his own interpretations of this unique phenomenon. "This strange breed, the 'Retro-Scal', came into existence around about the 1982/3 period and was completely unexpected. Fashionistas had started to write about football fans in Designer clothing and The Face had printed their famous piece on 'Casuals' in 1983, so in many ways the 'Retro-Scal' was a reaction to this popularisation of a street culture that had bypassed magazines and social commentators from 1978 until 1983. Liverpool fashion terrorists had always had an elitist slant on things but it is too simplistic to state that this was a reaction to the new found fame of the 'Designer clad football fan'. To really understand this phenomenon it is important to look at Liverpool as a major import/export centre, a place where 'Drug Culture' and the music associated with it took a firm hold in the late 70s and early 80s. By the early 80s, 1982/83 to be precise, articles began to appear in the press explaining a new breed of underground well dressed football fans ignored up until now by the mainstream media. The London press dubbed these people 'Casuals' and soon every newspaper in the UK was on the lookout for these social terrorists bedecked in 'Lilywhites' supplied Designer clad Sportswear who were rampaging around the Country in organised gangs. It was around about this point that Liverpudlians decided enough was enough and the Retro-Scal was born.

Basically the 'Retro-Scal' look was a reaction to expensive sportswear and was epitomised by the 'Old Man look'. Bemused staff at Dunne & Co, a traditional Gentlemen's Outfitters in Liverpool, didn't know what had hit them as young Scallys demanded a Harris Tweed of the bottle green variety. The classic look would have been a Harris Tweed or green Barbour coat (before Sloane Rangers popularised Barbour coats, a look adopted by Italian Ultras) a Marks & Spencer lambswool crew neck with button collared shirt underneath, a pair of slightly faded jeans and Clarks suede boots, cord shoes/brogues or Stan Smith training shoes. Cardigans were worn as an alternative to the crew neck and cord jackets were also worn as fashion crazy youngsters unwittingly discovered 'the Sicilian peasant look', twenty years before Giorgio Armani. Coupled with a new found admiration for their fathers or even their grandfathers' wardrobe, they also looked back at the previous generations music collections. Graffiti sprang up everywhere and 'Pink Floyd' and especially 'The Wall' adorned many walls of the city as young pot smokers paid homage to their new found heroes. It didn't just stop at Floyd. Soon any group that you could 'buzz' off were sought and proclaimed as 'better'. Simon & Garfunkel. Supertramp, Bob Dylan, Neil Young, Roy Harper and Marillion to name but a few.

By 1983 heroin had taken hold in the working-class heartlands of the City and the inevitability of the Drug Culture and music collision was all too apparent. The Retro-Scal basically dressed down and hair tended to get a bit longer (a sort of John Power/ Zutons head) and criminal gangs confused the look as gangs of dippers adopted the 'Barbour Country look' so they could mingle at Ascot and Cheltenham and fill their coats' cavernous pockets.

Liverpool, which up until 1983 had been a haven for dope smokers, was hit by a tidal wave of 'smack'. Graffiti even appeared on walls 'Where has all the pot gone?' as a City shortage took hold. On the other hand 'heroin' was openly available for the first time. It is important to know that in those days nobody had ever heard of 'smack' and only very few people knew what it was. It was my job to know, as I was a 'Youth worker' at the time and specialised in drug issues.

I remember a very attractive girl, a barmaid in fact, who was taking a half-an hour break from working in a notorious pub in the Dovecot/Huyton area of Liverpool, chasing the dragon in one of the pubs alcoves. I asked her what she was doing and she replied its only 'Smack'. 'You mean heroin' I replied and she said 'nah it's something called smack but you don't get addicted, you can take it or leave it, you don't inject it like heroin'. Oh the innocence of youth. I saw the girl several years later, her model like looks ravaged by the drug she thought she was in control of! Whether dealers had deliberately caused the pot shortage and promoted 'smack' as non-addictive is open for question but only 18 months after the worst civil disorder this country had ever witnessed heroin swamped the estates. 'Whisky to the Indians' was the first thing that came to mind.

This 83-86 period was the heyday of the Retro-Scal, fuelled by the Drug Culture and the music that went with it. The look was changing constantly from jeans to jumbo cords from tweed to cord jackets but the common denominator was that it was Label and Sportswear free. Think stereotypical Geography teacher look with a taste for all things Prog-Rock and you'll get the idea! Groups even emerged to cater for young Liverpudlians hunger for what was regarded by music journalists of the period as 'hippy music'. Groups like Groundpig became massive in the City playing a collection of Bob Dylan, Neil Young, Lindisfarne, Simon and Garfunkel, Cat Stevens and Peter Gabriel. Groundpig played at a 1000 capacity Bierkellar every Fri/Sat for about a two-year period, selling out the venue on most occasions with queues around the block and hundreds locked out. All the girls were 'glammed up' whereas most of the males looked as if they'd just come back from Glastonbury. This was a real youth phenomenon undocumented apart from one single article in The Face magazine called 'Dark side of The Mersey' by John McCready. James Brown who was working for the NME at the time and later went on to start 'Loaded' witnessed the scenes at a Groundpig concert and couldn't believe his eyes. The mayhem had a profound effect on him but he told me the NME couldn't cover it as no one will understand it or more importantly, believe it. John Peel who was DJ'ing at the same event called it 'absolutely extraordinary'."

A young David Miles worked in my wife Jeanette's work in the late 1980s. He became the subject of John McCready's Face magazine article which looked to capture Liverpools infatuation with Pink Floyd. At just 17 years old he had changed his name by deed poll to Floyd Miles, although his mother still called him David. In the article Floyd talks of 'Getting into' Pink Floyd just 6 months earlier but he had already spent £400 on records and had recently seen them at the now legendary Maine Road concert. Most of his days were spent looking through the second hand vinyl in Backtrax on Rainford Gardens next to Probe. His future plans included having a show on North Coast Radio which was run from the Bidston Estate where he lived. His intention was to just play Pink Floyd records.

I'm sure he would have had plenty of listeners on Merseyside.

A Legacy

Away from the haze of smoke and back to the terraces. The look that had been conceived four or five years earlier in Liverpool had now developed into a Nationwide obsession. Every Club in all four divisions had its own mob of Casual dressers. 'The wedge' was now the haircut of the masses. When rival firms battled outside of the grounds, it was hard to determine who was on whose side. The sight of 5/600 Scousers at away grounds had inspired many.

Aberdeen became the first Casual firm North of the Border, after noticing the Liverpool crew dressed up and without scarves at the European Cup game in October 1980. They had spent most of the game taking notes on the Scousers Casual attire. Before long they had christened themselves the A.S.C. [Aberdeen Soccer Casuals]. The same was happening up and down the land. On travelling to away games it was possible to see what each mob of supporters were wearing. They would only be a few yards away on the other side of a dividing fence.

The Manchester clubs were quick to catch onto the latest Culture and they would become known as 'Perry Boys' after the Fred Perry T-Shirts worn by all. Ian Hough in his book 'Perry Boys' recalls those first years 'It was 1979, it was only about the fifth time in the past year that I'd even heard the word 'Perry'. I was a thirteen-year-old doing my best to turn up in decent gear. I felt that Perries were definitely something, while not exactly being whatever it was I was trying to be, which had an inextricable football connection.' Ian goes on to mention an incident in the Stretford End one Saturday during the 1979/80 season. 'From nowhere, a couple of young lads made a beeline for me and Sid, but seemed unsure what to say to us once within speaking distance. They were small and skinny, but bigger than we were, probably around sixteen years old. Their hair was very 'Perry'.

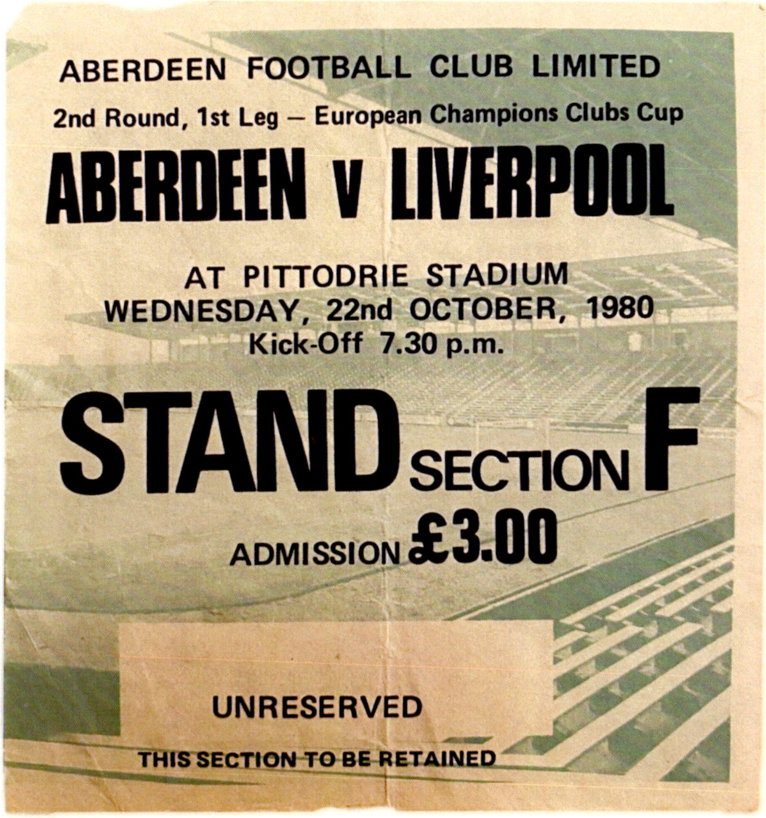
ABERDEEN FOOTBALL CLUB LIMITED
2nd Round, 1st Leg – European Champions Clubs Cup
ABERDEEN v LIVERPOOL
AT PITTODRIE STADIUM
WEDNESDAY, 22nd OCTOBER, 1980
Kick-Off 7.30 p.m.
STAND SECTION F
ADMISSION £3.00
UNRESERVED
THIS SECTION TO BE RETAINED

Period return
2nd
0690
OUT WED. 22ND OCT. 1980
RET WED/THURS 22ND/23RD OCT 1980
Liverpool Lime Street
to
ABERDEEN AND BACK
Valid only on advertised special
football trains
For conditions see over (M)
0690

They had burgundy hair and polo shirts with hoops around them, sleeves stretched down over their hands for gloves, and straight jeans. I could now see that the little green patch on their heels contained a white adidas logo, with the words 'Stan Smith' written under it. Evidently they thought we were from Liverpool, like them.'

Word was spreading in one way or another, whether it was Scousers visiting other parts of the Country or even your local Asian market trader who had a stall in St Johns market. Erics sister worked in St Johns Market in Liverpool 'The Asians who ran the market stalls in Liverpool, all lived in Manchester. I'm sure they returned to Manchester to tell their brethren who worked in the Arndale Centre tales of how many straight jeans they had sold in a week to all these young Scouse lads and girls. They would always knock up similar copies of top selling makes as well. Four stripe copies of adidas Cagoules as well as copies of Campri Ski Coats and Jockey Jackets.'

It took a while before the Cockneys discarded their flight jackets and let their hair grow out of a Skinhead. One or two Clubs do claim to have been onto the scene by the start of the decade but with London having such a large scope, it would take many months for word to spread. Once it happened though they would be christened 'Chaps'. Collectively the word 'Casuals' is now used to describe all.

London based DJ, Promotor and Boys Own Productions founder Terry Farley 'Arsenal were definitely the first London firm to dress en masse. I was really into the whole Liverpool thing you know. I got into The End magazine and I actually liked the Liverpool style of dressing. I was probably the only person at Chelsea who wore Trimm-Trabs and the only person who wore strap over trainers. I really liked that look. To be honest with you I think it was like 1984 when Chelsea came back up to the First Division and by then I think the Scousers were wearing cords and hunting jackets and dressing down. London have never really done dressing down very well, they like looking flash and they like showing how much they've spent on something.'

Although the 'Retro-Scal' look was about, many of the younger lads still hankered after that piece of Designer Sportswear no one else had, or at least Wade Smith didn't have. For many this still meant travelling abroad. A few firms were now travelling to Europe on a regular basis to pick up Designer wears to flog back home. Besides the sportswear, big name Italian Designers such as Armani were now being brought in. The whole world of International Designers was now opening up to the Youth back home. Those who did go to Europe regularly were at the leading edge of a Liverpool retail market, setting standards for the shops back home to follow. In 1980 the time-honoured tradition for Independent stores was to approach manufacturers such as Ben Sherman, Fred Perry etc. to stock their goods or to go to a retail exhibition show in Paris. Britain was in the midst of a recession and with there being no Brand Agencies set up in the UK at the time, Continental Brands were seldom approached due to the expense of travelling to Europe for their acquisition and a fluctuating Pound also meant the prices of foreign clothing was unstable and expensive. Throughout the course of the 80s these boundaries and borders would be broken down as fashions preoccupation with 'Casual' came to the forefront. Entrepreneurs with a taste for European designer wear began offering the retailers an abundance of goods.

As fervour spread, the foreign Brands soon realised the UK was at the cutting edge of a retail phenomenon. In a move that would lead to the mediocrity of the Culture, Agencies began opening in this Country to supply the Independent shops. Covetable, happening Labels once only available on an excursion to far off lands were soon available on the High Street.

Those lads who enjoyed the occasional sojourn to Europe would also look to take in the odd European game or Concert. After Liverpool's early exit from the European Cup in 1982, the only choice was to go and see Aston Villa in their European Cup Final against Bayern Munich in Rotterdam. England games seemed too risky for a pair of trainees. We picked a route that kept us clear of the Villa fans and so travelled through Belgium to Dusseldorf in Germany for the obligatory trainees and then back via Holland, taking in the match and picking up a couple of Tennis tops in Amsterdam en-route home. A Fila Polo T-Shirt, Fila shorts and an Adidas Lendl jumper were acquired from a goldmine of a Sport Shop in the back-streets of the Dam. The Tennis look of that summer was just in its infancy. On the journey via Belgium, we ended up sharing the train with a bunch of supporters who got on at Brussels. Their team, Racing Club Gent had just won the Belgium Premier League Cup. We decided to jump off at Gent with these supporters as we thought it should be pretty lively in the Town that night. We weren't far wrong. After finding a decent hotel, which made a change from sleeping in the Tram Station like the night before, we hit the Town. The only lively place appeared to be a small pub full of scarf waving, raucous fans of the local team. We made ourselves at home and duly joined in the celebrations. Some local hospitality meant free ale all night and then just on midnight a guy appears with a huge Cup. For the next hour everyone was drinking Champagne out of the proper Belgian Cup. [shades of Phil Thompson's trip to the Falcon with the European Cup I thought]. Next day Rotterdam and bunking into the Stadium involved us using the discarded stubs on the floor, ripped off by the ticket inspectors, then getting a Villa fan to pass the other half through the railings method. Those Villa fans that asked why we were there all got the same answer, 'It's a Liverpool thing, European football, clothes and trainees. etc'.

The summer of 1982 is best remembered for the afore-mentioned 'Tennis Look'. Many lads sported the look in Liverpool City Centre during a glorious Summer. Dressed like the tennis stars of the day, minus the racquet, the lads matched their mainly white Tacchini and Fila polo t-shirts with tennis shorts and socks. adidas trainers were still the obligatory favourite footwear.

Everyone in Liverpool now knew the gear was from abroad and so everyone's Summer holiday this year entailed visits to high fashion Continental stores for the latest sportswear. Even young teenagers on school trips to Europe were on the look out for the latest 'trabs' as they had nicknamed these new adidas imports. Tony was in Germany in '81 on an Anfield Junior Football League tour, but the main priority was to get a pair of adidas Comfort strap-overs like all the older kids were wearing back home.

As the styles engulfed the U.K. the look became fragmented as different regions took on their own interpretations of the Casual look. A Club orientated style wars took place with each set of supporters having their own take on the fashion. Up and down the Country entrepreneurs were taking a lead from Wade Smith and opening up shops selling Designer Sportswear. Even those shops usually associated with being Gentleman's Outfitters found out more money was able to be made from selling sportswear to the Youth of the day. The downside for the innovators was this enabled every punter to purchase the latest look. Therefore, the only option was to go for the most expensive. Suddenly 'Loadsamoney' Cockneys were jumping off the train head to toe in Burberry and then the late 80s arrived with Stone Island and C.P.Company. Designer Massimo Osti rubbed his hands with glee as his £500 coats landed on these shores. England fans rampaged through Europe picking up whatever was available with a compass patch. A Culture that had started off with cheap jeans and trainers had evolved into a monster. Youngsters with highly disposable incomes were only too willing to part with a month's wages for the jumpers and coats. The Thatcherite materialism of the 1980s would take us through into the 90s.

The Stone Island label became the Terrace label of the 90s. Football and Fashion now went hand in hand. The label meant 'Football Hooligan' to a lot of people and many night Clubs down South wouldn't allow people in wearing the compass patch. The Casual Culture had spiralled out of control. It's unfortunate that many people today think of Casuals and associate it with football hooliganism.

In reality this is not the truth. The truth lies on Merseyside were it was about 'image'. The image and look was everything. It was a Terrace fashion that transformed into a new Culture and although hooliganism had blighted the period, the Culture was happening because of Liverpools involvement in European Competition. It wasn't a hooligan uniform, it was Terrace fashion from the teenagers of Liverpool.

The 'Casual look' started with the trainers. It was a trainer obsession that grew to take in sportswear and then Designer clothing. Prior to adidas Samba there was no Casual. The Culture was wanting the newest, most exclusive trainers before anyone else. The Culture grew on Merseyside due to the fact that Liverpool played in Europe and so the fans travelled and brought back adidas trainers that were too expensive for a recession hit U.K. market. Once the trainers were more readily available, it was the sportswear that excited people.

The look of the late 70s defined a generation. The influence can be seen all around in the way shops such as Wade Smith developed and expanded throughout the 80s and 90s. Sportswear isn't just sold in Sports Shops anymore. The high street is full of shops stocking their own take on leisurewear as it became known. Whereas Sports Shops were few and far between in the 1980s, today you would find it hard to walk down a City Centre Street without passing 4 or 5 Stores selling training shoes and tracksuits.

Lads Mags such as Arena and Loaded sprung up in the 80s and 90s to sell us the Culture. Those initial Designer labels such as Prada, Hugo Boss, Giorgio Armani and many others started introducing sports labels as part of their make up and began manufacturing trainers so as not to miss out on the boom.

Purist Sports Companies such as adidas, Nike and Reebok joined the leisure industry in the 80s with adidas wholesale distribution alone rising from £30 million in 1983 to £300 million in the space of 15 years. Although uncomfortable with selling for leisure, adidas had to acknowledge the fact that the industry had grown beyond comprehension.

Counterfeiting became big business throughout the 80s as the latest names and labels were copied. The pricey status symbols were too expensive for many kids parents and a bit of 'blag gear' was the only option. The label moved from the inside of the clothing to the outside.

The bigger the name on the front of the T-shirt the better, it all became very ostentatious, but it all boiled down to the fact that this generation wanted the best and they wanted everyone to know they had it. Everyone became a walking advert. The logo label had to be seen. Lacoste were the first company to put the logo on the front of a shirt in the 1930s. Now every clothing company has a logo somewhere on the outside. One lad even bought Lacoste socks and unpicked the crocodiles so that he could sew them onto the front of his cheap t-shirts. Fila and Lacoste logos were being snipped from garments in shops by kids who couldn't afford them, so they could re-sow them onto cheap jumpers and shirts. Peer pressure was affecting everyone.

Today the high street has seen the demise of stylish individuality. Today's shoppers are spoilt for choice with nearly all of the shops having the same product. There is no need to traipse from one store to another. A co-ordinated purchase can be made from one shop or online and not necessarily one style either, mix and match from a cross section of designs and tastes is available from most stores.

The Terrace Culture hasn't just died though. It is still alive and evolving. Whereas the clothing of other Youth Cultures would make you look like you were going to a fancy dress party, the Casual Culture has evolved over the last four decades and is still very much a part of football and every day life. Not wanting to be force-fed fashion and mediocrity, today's stylish individual may hanker after an original pair of adidas trainees from the 80s, or maybe some top quality jacket, which may only be available from a select few outlets. Having a penchant for individuality and personal pride he would prefer to make a statement of his own identity and personality rather than wear the latest commodified styles.

The last great revolution in men's clothing began all those years ago on the streets of Liverpool. For the time being there has been nothing to compare.

EPILOGUE

As has been said, Casual as a culture is still alive. In almost two decades since 'The Liverpool Boys are in Town' was first published we have seen a massive resurgence in the 'Terrace Style' that was first witnessed in late 1970s Liverpool. The term is used loosely as I'm not talking about Lois Jeans and Pringle Jumpers but I'm talking about a predominant style worn particularly by those who frequent their local Stadium on a Saturday [Sunday, Monday etc etc]. A unique style that has worked in reverse and actually influences the fashion industry rather than the other way around.

Fashion isn't afraid to be associated with Football any more. Gone is the hooliganism that every clothing label had contempt for and was worried about being associated with. Nowadays the Casual is seen as some sort of useful commodity by the industry and one that it will willingly embrace. Hence, a brand such as adidas re-issuing an array of retro trainers that would fall apart on a Tennis Court but look very smart on the Terraces. They don't mind being associated with films such as Awaydays or The Firm. adidas aren't the only guilty ones, as the last 15 years has seen countless Fila and Tacchini re-issues made available, as well as iconic jackets made famous because they had been worn on the Terraces.

Apart from the major Brands selling a lifestyle back to the football supporter, new labels have come onto the scene that were launched to inspire lads to take pride in that sub-culture with which we were all a part of. The 80s Casuals label, set up in 2003, was probably the first original Terrace Brand solely set up to serve those of a similar unique identity. Many more Independent Brands have followed. It is so easy nowadays for entrepreneurs to be easily influenced and to begin their own label overnight. The Casuals Culture has spawned a new generation of would-be experts on the scene.

The influence of those first travellers to Europe in the 1970s and 80s are still having a major impact on the high street and on the football terraces of this fair land. Those globetrotters now own Clothing Labels, run Brand Agencies, open Menswear Stores, write Books and make Films. The Culture may have gone unnoticed by many, but it has now seeped into the mainstream. Some Clothing Labels turn over a million £'s, whilst Stores and Customers as far away as Japan and Germany order T-Shirts as the Culture attains a Global following.

Another aspect of Casual Culture that has evolved over the last 20 years but which seems to have been missed again by the media and magazines is the Art that has been inspired by the clothing worn on the Terraces. 'Terrace Culture' is an Art form that emerged in the early 2000's in the UK. Challenging the traditions of Fine Art in a way not dissimilar to Pop Art.

Emerging in the late 1950s and early 1960s, Pop Art challenged the traditions of Fine Art by using Popular Culture such as Comics, Advertising and mass consumed goods in its imagery. The 'Terrace Culture' artists attribute their work to a 1970/80s upbringing, with inspiration born on the Terraces of Football Grounds around the Country. Influences emerge, not from the football stars on the field, but from the clothing worn by fans at the time whilst attending the match. The Cultural scene of wearing sportswear [trainers, tracksuits, mountaineering jackets etc] as everyday wear rather than just for sport, plays a major factor in the Art, blurring the boundaries between the 'Low' Culture of items such as Training Shoes to make them 'High' Art as in a Dave White painting.

Employing techniques including Painting, Video and Graphic Illustration, the Art also includes subject matter from a childhood that was also open to numerous Sub-Cultures, new music and 'Coming of age' films, such as Mods, Skinheads, Two-Tone and Madchester, The Warriors, Quadrophenia etc as well as the game of Subbuteo and the burgeoning Computer games of the period. This may be the first time you'll have realised how much the Culture has seeped into our everyday lives but i can guarantee it wont be the last.

In 1999 the Tate Gallery in Liverpool held an exhibition entitled 'Remix'. Among the exhibits was a video installation by Mark Leckey titled intriguingly 'Fiorucci made me Hardcore'. For those of us old enough to remember Fiorucci in its heyday, we think of halcyon days on the terraces in the early 80s. Fiorucci jeans and sweatshirts obviously made its mark on some.

Mark Leckey was born in Birkenhead in 1964 and followed Everton home and away in the 1980s. Leckey's Youth has had a massive effect on his artistic adult life as memories of such times as being a Casual and watching Joy Division in Erics have resurfaced in his work. 'Fiorucci made me Hardcore' charts the rise of British Youth Cultures. Starting off in the 70s with video clips of Northern Soul dancers. The shift of styles and sound underlines the change in the Cultural landscape. The video climaxes after 15 minutes with scenes of acid house raves from the early 90s. Set to Marks own soundtrack, a voice over takes us through an array of designer brands championed by Casuals throughout the 1980s. Mark 'I remember when I was about 17 coming down to London with a small crew and going into Burberry. This bunch of no-mark kids from up North, and we knew exactly what we wanted which really threw the staff and customers in there. It was like a far more sophisticated punk'.

'Fiorucci....' is now regarded as the first contemporary Art piece to acknowledge the Casual scene. Mark went on to win the 2008 Turner Prize.

In 2003 the 80s Casuals Label came up with a simple idea to produce T-Shirts with iconic 1980s adidas trainers on the front aimed solely at lads who went to the match. The idea was to transport them back to those halcyon days with the iconic imagery. This simple idea evolved over the years and collaborations with epochal 80s brands Fila and Ellesse soon followed. The graphic designs became integral to 80s Casuals image and as more Brands followed along the 'Terrace Culture' path, illustrators and designers started producing prints of 80s trainers.

Before long major Brands such as adidas and Ellesse started using the key illustrators for projects of their own. 'The Art of the Terraces' was becoming commercialised and a new Art style had started to blossom.

Back in the real Art World Liverpool born Dave White, who had gained a BA in Fine Art at Liverpool John Moores University, produced a series of paintings titled 'Clash of the Titans' in 2003 for a major Exhibition at the Exposure Gallery in London. The Titans being adidas and Nike trainers. This pioneering Exhibition began a 'Sneaker Art' movement. The work offered an interesting viewpoint on street Culture by using a medium often associated with tradition and establishment. The subject of trainers being a part of disposable modern Culture, but in reality they hold a great deal of relevance in today's society. Besides an Andy Warhol 'Puma Invader' painting from 1985 hanging in the San Francisco MOMA the humble training shoe had never appeared as the sole object of affection on canvas. Within a couple of years of the London Exhibition Nike and the Jordan brand were collaborating with Dave on Training Shoes. Dave's paintings now retail for £10s of thousands.

Another Artist, Sheffield born Pete McKee regularly features football in his work, but again it's not the stars on the pitch. Pete draws on his Youth that saw a diverse array of sub-Cultures walking the streets, from Mods, Punks, Skinheads and the newly emerging Casuals. His Art pays homage to these Cultural tribes as well as a long lost pub life where tobacco filled the air or a teenage bedroom with a collection of vinyl records. Endorsements have come from the likes of The Arctic Monkeys and Oasis whilst commissions from Sir Paul Smith, Clarks Boots and Acme Studios have raised his profile.

Recent Terrace Culture Art seeping into the mainstream has seen visual artist Seana Gavin create amazing collages titled 'Sportswear Nomads' for the launch of the adidas Paris Trainers in Liverpool's Sevenstore. The commission included several photos, within the collages, from European trips we went on in the early 80s.

2022 will see 'Terrace Culture' Art take centre stage with a major Exhibition, accentuating a once chastised sub-Culture into the upper echelons of the Art World.

The 80s Casuals have come a long way from that first pair of adidas Samba.

The 80s Casuals have come a long way from that first pair of adidas Samba.